Routledge Revivals

God and Man in Early Israel

First published in 1956, *God and Man in Early Israel* deals with Old Testament history from Abraham to Solomon in the light of modern archaeological research and biblical scholarship, and in terms of the Christian belief in divine revelation. The book is divided into three parts—God and Man in the stories of the Patriarchs; God and Man in the making of a Nation; and God and Man in the founding of a Kingdom. Biblical references are given throughout the book. *God and Man in Early Israel* is intended as a companion to the study of the Bible, not as a substitute for it. It will be a fascinating read for students and researchers of religion, history, and classics.

God and Man in Early Israel

J. W. D. Smith

First published in 1956
by Methuen & Co. Ltd

This edition first published in 2024 by Routledge
4 Park Square, Milton Park, Abingdon, Oxon, OX14 4RN

and by Routledge
605 Third Avenue, New York, NY 10017

Routledge is an imprint of the Taylor & Francis Group, an informa business

© 1956 J. W. D. Smith

All rights reserved. No part of this book may be reprinted or reproduced or utilised in any form or by any electronic, mechanical, or other means, now known or hereafter invented, including photocopying and recording, or in any information storage or retrieval system, without permission in writing from the publishers.

Publisher's Note
The publisher has gone to great lengths to ensure the quality of this reprint but points out that some imperfections in the original copies may be apparent.

Disclaimer
The publisher has made every effort to trace copyright holders and welcomes correspondence from those they have been unable to contact.

A Library of Congress record exists under LCCN: 56003710

ISBN: 978-1-032-88823-1 (hbk)
ISBN: 978-1-003-53994-0 (ebk)
ISBN: 978-1-032-88846-0 (pbk)

Book DOI 10.4324/9781003539940

GOD AND MAN
IN EARLY ISRAEL

by

J. W. D. SMITH
M.A., Ed.B., D.D.
Jordanhill Training College

With 5 Maps and some Questions

METHUEN & CO. LTD
36 Essex Street, Strand, London, W.C.2

First published in 1956

CATALOGUE No. 8119/U

*Printed in Great Britain by J. W. Arrowsmith Ltd, Bristol
and bound by The Fisher Bookbinding Co. Ltd, London*

PREFACE

This book has been written to the requirements of one of the 'O' level syllabuses in Religious Knowledge set in the G.C.E. Examination of the Associated Examining Board. Thanks to the imaginative lines on which this syllabus, *God's Revelation of His Purpose in Old Testament History*, has been drawn up, the book should also serve other needs.

It deals with Old Testament history from Abraham to Solomon in the light of modern archaeological research and biblical scholarship, and in terms of the Christian belief in divine revelation. The author realises that some of his readers may be genuinely sceptical of a divine purpose in human history, and he attempts to meet this difficulty as best he can within the limits his commission has imposed.

Biblical references are given throughout, and, it need hardly be said, the book is intended as a companion to the study of the Bible, not as a substitute for it.

J. W. D. S.

CONTENTS

PART I

GOD AND MAN IN THE STORIES OF THE PATRIARCHS

1.	New light on the Patriarchs	3
2.	Abraham, the man of faith	5
3.	Jacob, later named Israel	14
4.	Joseph, and his brothers	24

PART II

GOD AND MAN IN THE MAKING OF A NATION

5.	Moses, the prophetic leader and lawgiver	34
6.	Joshua, military leader and missionary	52

PART III

GOD AND MAN IN THE FOUNDING OF A KINGDOM

7.	Samuel, religious leader in time of crisis	62
8.	David the warrior	74
9.	David the king	84
10.	Solomon: builder of the Temple	99

EPILOGUE

Does the Story reveal a Purpose?	111
SOME QUESTIONS	117
INDEX	121

MAPS

The world of the Patriarchs	4
From Egypt to Canaan	45
Joshua's entry into Canaan	53
Israel in the time of Samuel and Saul	66
The kingdom of David	87

Part I

GOD AND MAN
IN THE STORIES OF THE PATRIARCHS

CHAPTER 1

NEW LIGHT ON THE PATRIARCHS

THE religious faith of the Jewish people began with the events of the Exodus and the teaching of Moses. The God of whom the Old Testament speaks is always 'the LORD thy God who brought thee out of the land of Egypt, from the house of bondage' (cf. Deut. v. 6; see also Exod. xx. 2; Joshua xxiv. 17). But the writers of the Bible were familiar with earlier stories. They knew that their ancestors had come long, long ago from the land of the two rivers. There were stories of Abraham, the first ancestor of their people, and of Isaac his son. There were stories of Jacob, whose name was changed to Israel, and of the twelve sons who gave their names to the tribes known as 'the children of Israel'. These stories told how the Hebrews had first come to Palestine and how some of them had found their way into Egypt and had become slaves there. Abraham, Isaac, Jacob and Joseph had lived long before Moses but the Bible writers were quite sure that the LORD, who had delivered their people from Egypt, had been leading their earlier ancestors from the very beginning.

It used to be doubted whether these patriarchs were real individuals. It was suggested that the stories told about them might really be popular legends which had been used to explain the origin and early history of different tribes and peoples. The stories of Jacob and Esau, for instance, might have been told to explain the rivalry and enmity between their supposed descendants, the Israelites and the Edomites. Or some of the stories told of individuals might have been originally episodes in the history of tribes. Such suggestions may have some truth in them. The stories of the patriarchs seem more like folk tales from a distant past than reliable records of historical occurrences. It is difficult to believe that details of incident and conversation survived through centuries before they were committed to writing.

4 GOD AND MAN IN EARLY ISRAEL

Twentieth-century evidence from archaeology has thrown new light on this subject. It has been discovered that the social and religious customs which we meet in the stories of the patriarchs belong to the period to which the stories refer. It seems strange to us, for instance, that Abraham, before he had a son, should have regarded Eliezer, his chief servant, as his heir rather than his nephew Lot. (Gen. xv. 2–3, R.V.) But the discovery of the *Nuzu Tablets* in Iraq in 1925 showed that this was a recognized social custom in these far-off times. Such a detail can hardly have been invented by a writer of the ninth century B.C., to whom it must have seemed as strange as it does to us. Evidence such as this has strengthened the belief that Abraham and Jacob, at least, were real individuals round whom many stories and legends gathered in popular tradition.

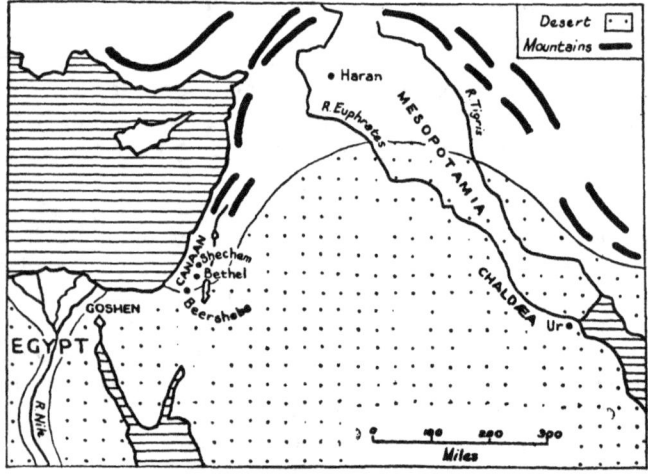

The world of the Patriarchs

CHAPTER 2

ABRAHAM: THE MAN OF FAITH

Abraham's Early Home (Gen. xi. 27–32)

The Bible tells us that Abraham, or Abram, as he was called at first, was born in Ur of the Chaldees and went to Haran with his father Terah. From Haran he migrated to Canaan (as Palestine was called in the early days) and settled there. He also paid a visit to Egypt during a time of famine. We cannot be sure when this journey from Haran took place. Students of the Old Testament differ considerably in the dates they suggest. Some would say that Abraham entered Canaan soon after 2000 B.C. Others would put his journey as late as 1750 B.C. We cannot expect to be very accurate without more evidence than we have at present.

Abraham travelled by a well-worn route. The early ancestors of the Jews were Semites. They belonged to that branch of the human race which is named after Shem, the son of Noah. The original home of the Semites is believed to have been the Arabian desert but constant movement seems to have taken place, over a period of many centuries, from the desert homeland into more fertile areas. Kindred peoples of Semitic stock moved in search of pasture into the valley of the Euphrates or, through Syria and Palestine, towards the valley of the Nile. During two thousand years or more, this whole region was gradually peopled by Semitic tribes. The Jewish people belong to this racial stock, although it is the modern Arabs, rather than the Jews, who show the physical characteristics of these early Semitic peoples. The typical features of the Jew are probably due to intermarriage with the Hittites, from Asia Minor, at an early stage in their history.

It would seem, then, as if Abraham and his family formed but one group among many ancient travellers on that same route. The others were migrating for political and economic reasons but it was remembered of Abraham that he went at the call of God.

Ur and Haran were important cities in these distant days. The archaeologists have dug down into the earth and uncovered many relics of ancient civilizations in the lands we now know as Syria and Iraq. They have shown that Abraham must have spent his early life in contact with the most highly civilized life of his day. The inhabitants of Ur and Haran must have included many wealthy and cultured people. In leaving Haran, Abraham may have been turning his back on a life of comfort and security and he was certainly facing a much more rigorous and insecure existence when he set off westwards towards an unknown land.

Ur and Haran were centres of moon-worship in those days and there is an old Jewish legend which tells how Abraham rejected the worship of the heavenly bodies. It is preserved in the Koran, the sacred book of the Mohammedans. 'And thus did we show Abraham the kingdoms of the Heavens and of the Earth, that he might be established in knowledge. And when the night overshadowed him, he beheld a star. "This", said he, "is my Lord": but when it set, he said, "I love not gods which set." And when he beheld the moon uprising, "This," said he, "is my Lord": but when it set, he said, "Surely, if my Lord guide me not, I shall surely be of those who go astray." And when he beheld the sun uprise, he said, "This is my Lord; this is greatest." But when it set, he said, "O my people! I share not with you the guilt of joining gods with God; I turn my face to him who hath created Heavens and the Earth, following the right religion: I am not one of those who add gods to God."' (The Koran: Everyman edition: p. 324.)

Abraham hears God's Call (Gen. xii. 1–9)

This old legend, and the information which the archaeologists have given us, help us to realize what kind of man Abraham may have been and to imagine what thoughts may have been in his mind as he set off on his momentous journey. He was apparently dissatisfied with life as he found it around him. All the splendours of that ancient civilization failed to satisfy him. The religious beliefs and practices of the moon-worshippers did not meet his deepest needs. He felt that human life could be finer and more satisfying than he had found it in the cultured society in which his youth had been spent. He longed for some more satisfying answer to his deepest questionings than the priests of the moon cult could offer. As the writer to the Hebrews puts it he was seeking 'a city which hath foundations whose builder and maker is God' (Heb. xi. 10). And that deep unsatisfied desire was like a voice from the unseen calling him to leave the familiar, comfortable secure life of Haran behind him and go out in search of a new land and a new way of life and worship.

'So Abram departed as the LORD had spoken to him'. These simple words sum up the picture which the Bible gives us of Abraham. He was a man who had learned to recognize God's voice. There would be other voices that counselled him to stay in Haran. His friends probably urged him to stay. His wife and relations may have been unwilling to leave Haran. Probably he had many hesitations and misgivings himself. But the voice that bade him go awakened response at the deepest levels of his nature and he knew that it was the voice of God.

Did God really speak to Abraham?

How did Abraham know it was the voice of God? And was he right? There is no simple answer to these questions. There have been false prophets who have said: 'Thus saith the Lord', deceiving themselves and other people. In Jeremiah xxviii, we read of a public disagreement between two 'prophets'. One was Jeremiah himself and the other was a man called Hananiah. Each used the phrase 'Thus saith the Lord', but they give opposite advice to the people of Judah. Hananiah told them that Babylonian power would be broken and the Jewish captives set free. Jeremiah said that the people of Judah must be content to accept the yoke of Babylonia.

One thing is quite clear. The manner in which a revelation comes does not determine whether it comes from God. No vision or dream or audible voice can guarantee that God is speaking. Such experiences may form part of a genuine revelation from God but they may also be evidence of mental illness. The Bible constantly uses the phrase 'God said to . . .' but these words describe the inner certainty of the experience. They do not necessarily imply that a voice was actually audible. Abraham may have heard an audible voice but there is no reason to believe that he did. And even if he had done so our question would still be unanswered.

The story of Jeremiah and Hananiah may help us. Looking back now we can see clearly that Hananiah was wrong and Jeremiah was right. Hananiah believed that God would always look after the people of Judah and overthrow their enemies. To him God was a supernatural ally who could be counted on to support Judah's interests in all circumstances.

When Hananiah spoke to the people he was telling them what they wanted to hear. It was not the voice of God that was speaking. It was the voice of self-centred national desires and hopes. Jeremiah's advice was quite different. It was wrung from him against all the desires and hopes of his Jewish heart. He, too, would gladly have seen Babylonia defeated and the Jewish captives restored to their homes but the voice of God spoke more loudly, for him, than the voice of human desire.

Here, then, is part of the answer to our question. The voice of God and the voice of selfish human desire do not often say the same thing. If they seem to do so we should be hesitant about believing that it is really God who is speaking. Jeremiah drew attention to this truth when he said to Hananiah: 'The prophet which prophesieth of peace, when the word of the prophet shall come to pass, then shall the prophet be known, that the LORD hath truly sent him'. (Jer. xxviii. 9.)

But there are other difficulties. Abraham himself believed, at a later stage in his life, that God was telling him to sacrifice his son Isaac. That was certainly not the voice of selfish desire yet surely Abraham was wrong in thinking that it was the voice of God? It would seem, therefore, that men have had to learn to recognize the voice of God. Theologians explain this

ABRAHAM: THE MAN OF FAITH 9

by saying that men's knowledge of God has been dulled and distorted by the fact that men have distrusted and disobeyed their maker, and have allowed self-will to rule their lives. God has never ceased speaking to men but men have either misunderstood or deliberately disobeyed His will. The Old Testament tells of men who heard God speak and who obeyed but even they did not always understand very clearly and they did not always obey perfectly. It is only in Jesus Christ that we find perfect understanding and perfect obedience. That is part of what we mean when we call him 'Son of God'.

It was certainly not self-interest that urged Abraham to leave a comfortable home in Haran and to brave the hazards of a long journey across the desert to an unknown land. Abraham had an inner certainty that God Himself was speaking and that inner certainty gave him the courage and confidence which he needed. He knew that God could be trusted and he knew also that God must be obeyed.

Trust and obedience are essential features in the Biblical picture of Abraham. In the New Testament his story is even used to illustrate the attitude of Christian faith, or trust. (Heb. xi. 1, 8.) In obeying God's call to leave Haran, Abraham committed himself to God without hesitation or condition. He went out 'not knowing whither he went'. Looking back over many centuries we can see the outcome of his act of faith, as he could not, and we can recognize that it was fruitful beyond his dreams. Did God really speak to Abraham? The words of Jesus point us towards the best answer to our question: 'Do men gather grapes of thorns, or figs of thistles? . . . Wherefore by their fruits ye shall know them'. (Matt. vii. 15–20.)

Abraham's self-forgetful generosity (Gen. xiii.)

The qualities of trust and obedience are illustrated in the other familiar stories of Abraham. Only a man who trusted God utterly could act with the generosity shown in Abraham's dealings with his kinsman Lot. Well-watered pasture land is !a necessity of existence to nomadic shepherds. Abraham and Lot needed food and water for their flocks and herds and their servants were quarrelling because there was not enough pasture land available. Abraham suggested to Lot that they should divide the land between them and separate in order to avoid constant bickering between their servants. Abraham was the senior and he might well have chosen the best of the land for himself but, with self-forgetful generosity, he gave the first choice to Lot. Such action does not spring from a sense of duty. It is the action of a man whose life is so fully committed to God in trust and obedience that he is free from over-anxious concern about his own immediate needs. Abraham was ready to live as Jesus said that men should live (cf. Matt. vi. 31–4).

An heir is promised to Abraham (Gen. xv. 1–6)

Genesis xv., has some strange, but interesting, material in it. The first six verses tell us of a vision that came to Abraham, perhaps in a dream. Abraham was childless and, in accordance with the custom of his times, his heir was Eliezer, the chief servant of his household. Abraham had hoped and believed that he was to be the founder of a great nation that would bring blessing to all mankind. It was not just the emptiness of his own life which had troubled him in Haran. The life around him, in spite of all its wealth and splendour, seemed empty and meaningless. Surely, he had felt, man's life was meant to be finer and fuller than this. And the voice that spoke to him in Haran had seemed to promise that it would be so. His journey from Haran, he had felt certain, was full of rich possibilities for all future generations.

But Abraham was growing old and he had no son. Perhaps, as he lay down to sleep, he was feeling depressed and despondent. At any rate the story tells that, in his vision, he received the assurance that his descendants would be as numerous as the stars in the sky and this section of the chapter ends with the comment: 'And he believed in the LORD; and he counted it to him for righteousness'. The writer is drawing our attention to Abraham's unquestioning trust in God and he is reminding us that such trust is the foundation of all right living.

ABRAHAM: THE MAN OF FAITH

A Promise that cannot be broken (Gen. xv. 7–19)

The following verses contain the account of a strange primitive ceremony. This type of ritual was used in ancient times when men entered into a solemn agreement, or covenant, with one another. If either party failed to keep the covenant he laid himself open, it was believed, to the fate that had fallen upon the divided animals. In Jer. xxxiv. 18 there is a reference to men making such a covenant with God. In this passage it seems to be God who is expressing the certainty of his promises to Abraham through this solemn rite. Fire and smoke often figure in the Old Testament as signs of the divine presence and the passage therefore implies that God Himself passed between the divided pieces of the sacrifice. This, too, may have been a vision which came to Abraham in a dream and gave him further assurance of the certainty of God's promises. It is true, at least, that the writer who recorded this old story wanted us to realize that God had a purpose for the people of Israel from the very beginning of their history and that that purpose contained a promise which could not be broken.

Abraham and Ishmael (Gen. xxi. 1–21)

In Gen. xxi. 1–21 we read about Ishmael, the son of Abraham and Hagar, his wife's servant. The Bible writers knew stories which told of the ancestors of other people akin to themselves and they included these stories in their record. The Ammonites and the Moabites were said to be descended from Lot and Ishmael's descendants are said to have peopled the desert area in the north of the Sinai peninsula. The story of Hagar and Ishmael seems strange and cruel to us but it is quite in keeping with the customs of the times. The Nuzu tablets include a marriage contract which contains details which throw light on this old story. The bridegroom is not to take another wife unless his bride remains childless. If she has no children the bride must give her husband another wife from among her servants and the contract warns her that she must treat the children of such a wife in a humane way. Many wives seem to have felt, and acted, in the way that Sarah did. It is interesting to notice, however, that this story shows Abraham grieving over Ishmael and only allowing Sarah to do what she wishes because he believes that he can trust his child to God's care.

A severe test of Abraham's faith (Gen. xxii.)

In Gen. xxii we see Abraham's trust in God put to a very severe test. We are told that God commanded him to take the only son of his wife Sarah, kill him and burn his body as a sacrificial offering to God. This was Isaac, the child born to Abraham and Sarah when they were already old. This was the child through whose descendants all God's promises to Abraham were to be fulfilled. How could these promises be fulfilled if Isaac died? Yet God seemed to be demanding Isaac's death. The story is told simply and vividly. The successive phrases by which Isaac is described in the words of God's command to Abraham remind us of the father's feelings. Each phrase speaks with increasing poignancy of the severe test to which Abraham's religious devotion is being exposed. The repetition of the words 'they went both of them together' has a similar effect for they remind us of the lonely path by which Abraham expected to return and the full poignancy of the father's situation is exposed by Isaac's artless question about the sacrificial lamb. It is a moving story and it is told with great skill.

How should we understand this story? We cannot believe that God could make any such demand. Jesus has shown us the love of God for man. He has taught us to think of God as a loving Father. How can we possibly believe that God would expose a father to such a cruel ordeal? We can only understand this story if we try to put ourselves in Abraham's position. Child sacrifice was a common religious custom in Canaan at the time of Abraham. He must often have seen evidence of that practice and it would have been quite natural for a deeply religious man to feel his own devotion to God challenged by such a practice. Could he face such a test? Was his loyalty to God greater than his love for his son? Could he give back to God the life of the heir born to him in his old age?

Could he surrender his hope that God's promises would be fulfilled through Isaac and his descendants? When such questions arose in his mind they must have seemed like a supreme summons to trust and obedience. And Abraham knew that his response to God's claims must be unconditional and unquestioning.

There are many passages in the Old Testament which criticize the practice of child sacrifice. (See Lev. xviii. 21; Deut. xviii. 10; 1 Kings xvi. 34; 2 Kings xvi. 3, xxi. 6; Mic. vi. 6–8.) Such passages make it clear enough that the practice was not unknown among the Israelites themselves even as late as the seventh century B.C. It is quite possible that it was an accepted practice among the Hebrews in primitive times. Indeed the laws in the book of Exodus seem to point in this direction. According to Exod. xxii. 29 every first-born son was to be dedicated to God and other laws speak of the first-born sons being redeemed by some other offering. In the eyes of the Bible writers, however, child sacrifice was wholly evil. The prophet Micah expresses the true insight of Israel's prophetic faith when he says 'What doth the LORD require of thee but to do justly, to love mercy and to walk humbly with thy God'.

We should remember Micah's words when we read this old story. Abraham was mistaken in thinking that God wanted him to kill his son and burn his body as an act of worship. He had still to learn the truth which was so clear to Micah. He did not understand fully the nature of the God he worshipped. Yet the story does illustrate the true nature of religious faith. Abraham *believed* that God required this sacrifice of him and he was prepared to trust God utterly and to obey him without question. As he set out that day with Isaac he went out, as he did at Haran, 'not knowing whither he went'. He was making a supreme surrender of trust. And by his very act of trust and obedience he gained new insight. He learned that God did not require the death of his son. It is only by trying to do what we honestly believe to be God's will for us that we learn more of what God's will really is.

CHAPTER 3

JACOB, LATER NAMED ISRAEL

THE Bible tells us that the Israelites were descended from Jacob, whose name was changed to Israel, and that Esau was the ancestor of the Edomites. Some people think that the stories of Jacob and Esau describe, in story form, the relationships between these two kindred peoples who were neighbours and rivals for many centuries. Edom was the older nation. In Gen. xxxvi. 31-9 we are given a list of eight Edomite kings who reigned before the monarchy had been established among the Israelites. But the Israelites became a more important and a more powerful nation than Edom—just as Jacob secured the privileges that belonged by right of birth to his elder brother Esau. The stories of Jacob and Esau may therefore be regarded as hero-stories about the early leaders of two kindred peoples. They describe the characteristics and reflect the varying fortunes of the two nations and it is hardly possible to decide when we are reading about historical adventures of two individuals and when we are reading a story which describes the fortunes of two nations.

It must be remembered, however, that the Bible writers regarded Abraham, Isaac and Jacob as actual historical individuals who were the early ancestors of their people. As they retold the old traditions which had come down from the past they did so with a religious motive. They wanted to show how God had been dealing with their people from the earliest times. They retold the old stories, therefore, in the light of their own knowledge of God and they put their own religious meaning into them at many points. It is interesting for us to ask questions about the origin of the stories and to discuss whether the patriarchs were historical individuals but the answer to these questions—even if we could reach a certain answer—does not affect the religious value of the stories for us.

In order to appreciate their teaching we should read them as actual experiences of historical individuals.

Jacob the typical Israelite
Jacob is, in many ways, a much more real figure to us than Abraham. We can understand his motives and we can follow the development of his character. Abraham is the 'father of the faithful'. He is the ideal figure of the man of faith who trusts and obeys God at all times. The writers of the Old Testament looked back to Abraham as their first ancestor when they thought of themselves as the chosen people of God, called to play a great part in the purposes of God. He represents the ideal Israelite, the pattern to which all true Israelites should conform (cf. Luke xix. 9). But they were 'children of Israel' also and Jacob is a much more representative Israelite. In him we can trace many of the characteristics, both good and bad, which can be seen in the whole history of Israel.

This contrast makes the stories of Jacob far more interesting and more lifelike than the stories of Abraham. In the latter we see the ideal picture of the true relationship between man and God but the stories of Jacob show us a real human being with obvious faults and we are able to follow his spiritual pilgrimage at two critical stages of his life. If we try to visualize the actual circumstances of Jacob's life, as they are suggested to us by the Biblical story, we can understand his motives more clearly and see the meaning of the two great passages which tell how God spoke to him at these two turning-points in his experience.

Jacob and Esau (Gen. xxv. 21–6)
Jacob and Esau were twin sons of Isaac and Rebekah but Esau had been born first. Esau was a skilful hunter who loved the open air. He was his father's favourite son. Jacob was a quiet, home-loving shepherd whose interests drew him closer to his mother. Names are often very important in the Bible for, in olden times, men were often given names which described some distinctive physical feature or some marked

character trait. The word Esau is thought by some to be derived from an Arabic word meaning 'thick-haired' and Jacob's name is supposed to describe his character. It is supposed to mean one who takes by the heel, or supplants, another. There is a story in the Bible which tells that, when the twins were born, Jacob was holding on to his brother's heel as if he were trying to get in front of Esau.

The early Jacob is an unattractive character and most readers find that their sympathies are with his brother Esau. It is only when we look more closely at the two brothers that we can begin to see possibilities in Jacob, which were not present in Esau. The story of the birthright exposes the strength and the weakness of each of them. It is not easy for us to realize just how important the birthright was in nomadic shepherd society. The first-born son did not only inherit a larger share of the family possessions. He also inherited a position of dignity and privilege as the head of the family. In nomadic society this position had almost a religious significance. The tribal head was the heir of all the great achievements of the past and the guardian of future possibilities. Isaac's eldest son would occupy a position of special privilege and responsibility. Jacob and Esau must often have heard their father Isaac talk of the mysterious promises of God. With a little imagination we can picture Isaac telling the two boys of the strong urge which drew Abraham away from his early home in Haran, and of his great hope that God would use his heirs to lead all nations into the true way of life.

Both boys would hear these words but one listened with eager interest and the other paid little heed. Jacob had the imagination to realize the high honour and the great, if still mysterious, destiny that awaited Abraham's oldest son and he had sufficient ambition to wish that he, rather than Esau, might have been that first-born child. These envious longings would be strengthened by Esau's careless indifference. Esau had no interest in future possibilities. The immediate satisfactions of the moment were all that mattered to him.

This contrast shows the greater possibilities in Jacob's character. His imagination showed him the true nature of the privileges belonging to the eldest son and so he was the better fitted to inherit them. Even his ambition was a mark of his potential greatness. We can hardly wonder that he chafed at the thought that such high privileges must go to one who did not value them and could not, therefore, be expected to prove himself worthy of them.

Jacob's cunning (Gen. xxv. 27-34)

But it is impossible to justify Jacob's actions. He was true to his name. He was ready to seize any opportunity which might enable him to supplant his brother. He was ready even to use cunning and deceit to gain his ends. At first it was only cunning. Esau came in hungry and exhausted from a hunting expedition and found Jacob cooking a savoury meal of lentils. The sight and the smell of the food awakened an urgent demand from the hungry Esau. He was concerned, as always, with the satisfaction of immediate need and Jacob saw his opportunity. Having agreed to give Esau food in exchange for the birthright he made sure that Esau would not go back on the bargain when he had had time to think about it. Before Jacob would give Esau the food, Esau had to swear a solemn oath that Jacob would enjoy the rights and privileges of the eldest son.

Jacob's deceit (Gen. xxvii)

Cunning was followed by deceit. Esau's oath was binding on him but Jacob must have realized that Isaac would insist on giving his dying blessing to his oldest son. This blessing was the means by which the privileges of the birthright were bestowed on the heir. How could Jacob secure that blessing for himself? Cunning had secured the thoughtless consent of his brother but deceit was needed before his father could be persuaded to pronounce the coveted blessing on Jacob instead of Esau.

At this point in the story Rebekah came to the aid of her favourite son. Isaac was conscious of growing weakness and he had resolved to give his blessing to Esau before it was too late. He asked Esau to go out hunting and to prepare a savoury meal of venison so that Isaac might be strengthened for the ceremonial blessing. Rebekah persuaded Jacob to take his brother's place, relying on the failing senses of the old man, and to secure the dying man's blessing for himself. Jacob did so and the plan succeeded. 'Is not he rightly named Jacob' said Esau, 'for he hath supplanted (literally 'Jacob-ed') me these two times' (Gen. xxvii. 36)

Jacob at Bethel (Gen. xxviii.)

Rebekah learned that Esau, in his anger, was planning to kill Jacob as soon as their father was dead. She arranged, therefore, with Isaac that Jacob should be sent to seek a wife among their relatives who lived still in Haran, from which their ancestor Abraham had come many years before. Thus Jacob left his home in Beersheba and set out on the long, lonely road to Haran. As the sun set he happened to be in the vicinity of a shrine (Hebrew: 'the place': should probably be understood as a sacred place or shrine) and he lay down there to sleep.

Jacob's dream at Bethel was an occasion of deep religious meaning for him. It was a great turning point in the development of his character. In order to understand it aright we need to imagine the thoughts and feelings of Jacob as he lay down to sleep. He was a young man, going out to find a wife and to seek a fortune. As he travelled through the sun-lit hours his thoughts would be busy with his future plans and prospects and his heart would be full of hope. But other thoughts and feelings would crowd upon him with the hours of darkness. Memories of home would come back to him and, perhaps, a deeper realization of his situation as a guilty fugitive. He had risked so much to gain the privileges of the first-born and now he was an exile. He had shut himself out from his father's house. Had he perhaps cut himself off from his father's God? Would the strange god of this nearby shrine be friendly or unfriendly towards him? Feelings of loneliness and misgiving, mingled hopes and fears must have kept him awake and restless until physical weariness overcame him and he fell asleep. The hills in the neighbourhood of Bethel rise by rocky ledges, one above another, towards their summit. As his eyes

JACOB, LATER NAMED ISRAEL 19

were closing he would see these strange terraces of rock on the hillside rising like a great rocky stairway towards the sky.

As Jacob slept he dreamed. In his dream the rocky hillside became a great flight of steps stretching between earth and heaven, with angels passing up and down upon it. The word 'ladder' (Gen. xxviii. 12) suggests the wrong picture to our minds. The angels were passing each other, moving in opposite directions, on a broad stairway. As Jacob looked in awe at this evidence of his nearness to the spiritual world it seemed, in his dream, as if the God of his fathers were standing beside him and speaking to him. And the words were familiar words. Many a time Isaac had spoken these words as he told of God's mysterious promises to their ancestor Abraham. But this time they were addressed directly to Jacob and words of comfort and assurance were added to them. He was indeed to inherit these promises and the God of Abraham and Isaac would be with him to bless him and to bring him again to his father's home.

Jacob tries to bargain with God

And Jacob awoke and said: 'Surely the LORD is in this place and I knew it not'. The note of surprise in these words suggests that Jacob had shared the prevalent belief that every tribe had its own God whose power and influence did not extend beyond the tribal territory. But the awe in Jacob's words and the solemn vow which he swore show that the reality of God's presence had come home to him now as never before. Jacob must often have heard Isaac speak of God. He must have learned to worship along with Isaac at the altar at Beersheba. But this was different. At Beersheba he had known *about* God. At Bethel he felt God's very presence and he knew that God was speaking to him. From this time forward the God of his fathers was Jacob's God also.

Yet this experience had not changed the essential nature of the man. What he had heard God say to him was what he *wanted* to hear. Was God really speaking to Jacob through *all* the words of his dream? Were some of the words expressing his own selfish desires? God had certainly other things to say to Jacob which Jacob was not yet ready to hear. His heart was still set on the fulfilment of his own hopes and ambitions. The very vow in which he expressed his loyalty to the God of his fathers showed the essential nature of the man. In his anxiety to secure every possible advantage for himself he was ready even to make a bargain with God: '*If* God will . . . then shall the LORD be My God.' Jacob had still much to learn of God.

Jacob's love and loyalty towards Rachel (Gen. xxix. 1–30)

The story of Jacob's marriage to his cousin Rachel shows a finer side of his nature. She was the younger daughter of Laban, the brother of Rebekah. Jacob had been warmly welcomed by his mother's brother and had been received into the household as a member of the family. His quick emotional nature was stirred by this friendly reception and his affections were captured by the beauty of Laban's younger daughter. The eyes were an important feature in oriental standards of beauty and, apparently, Leah's eyes lacked the brilliant lustre of Rachel's. Jacob was penniless and he could not offer the customary bridal gift but he offered, instead, to give Laban seven years' service without wages. Laban accepted the offer and Jacob worked and waited seven years for his bride. 'And they seemed to him but a few days for the love he had to her'. These simple words show us very clearly the loyalty and devotion of which Jacob was capable.

When the seven years were over Jacob himself suffered from the same kind of deceitful behaviour that he had inflicted on others. It was contrary to eastern custom for a younger daughter to be married before her sister. Instead of explaining this difficulty at the beginning Laban had accepted Jacob's offer and, when the seven years were up, he deceived Jacob shamefully. The bride was heavily veiled throughout the marriage ceremony, in accordance with eastern custom, and Laban tricked Jacob into marrying Leah instead of Rachel. Jacob knew now what it felt like to be deceived. But his love and his loyalty were so great that he willingly agreed to serve another seven years that he might have Rachel also as his wife.

JACOB, LATER NAMED ISRAEL   21

Jacob is too cunning for Laban (Gen. xxxi.)

The finer side of Jacob's nature is certainly seen in his relationship with Rachel but the experience of being deceived did not cure Jacob of the habit of deceiving. Once the fourteen years of service were over Laban made a new bargain with Jacob but Jacob proved himself more cunning than his father-in-law in the art of deception. By deceit and cunning he enriched himself until his wealth in flocks and herds was greater even than Laban's. Laban grew resentful and his sons grew jealous. The time had come, it seemed to Jacob, for him to return to his father's home. Leah and Rachel went with Jacob and all their family servants and possessions. They went off secretly and Rachel carried away the household gods to bring them luck. Laban pursued them and Rachel tricked her father so that his accusation of theft was not proved. A friendly agreement was made between the two households and Jacob continued on his way.

Scholars think that this story of Jacob's return to Canaan with his eleven sons may point back to a second migration of Hebrew peoples from the old homeland in Haran. The early history of the Hebrews would certainly be much less simple than the Bible stories suggest and it is reasonable to suppose that traditions belonging to different branches of the early ancestral stock were handed down from ancient times and woven together into a single, continuous story by the Old Testament historians. These historians had a simple theme. They wanted to show how God had been leading their people even in these far-off times and they used such early traditions as were available to them to set forth that theme as simply and clearly as possible.

Jacob prepares to meet Esau (Gen. xxxii. 1–23)

The next part of Jacob's story brings us to a new crisis in his history. As he journeyed back to Canaan Jacob must have grown increasingly uneasy. He realized that he must now face the brother whom he had cheated of his inheritance twenty years before. He did not know what reception might await him and he took steps to propitiate and impress his brother.

He sent messengers to announce his arrival. He told the messengers to be most courteous and respectful but they were also to make it quite clear to Esau that Jacob was now no penniless fugitive but a man of great wealth and property.

The messengers returned with disturbing news. Esau was on his way to meet Jacob and he had four hundred men with him. Jacob's worst fears seemed to have been realized. It was evident that his brother had not forgiven or forgotten the wrongs he had suffered. In face of this danger Jacob acted with his old cunning. He divided his possessions into two companies in the hope of saving at least half of his property. And he sent further messengers to Esau. But this time they did not go empty-handed. He sent a number of servants in relays, with a succession of valuable presents, in the hope of appeasing his brother's anger. Then he left Leah and Rachel with his family and family servants on the north side of the river Jabbok while he himself awaited Esau on the south side.

Jacob's spiritual struggle and victory (Gen. xxxii. 24-32)

Before Jacob met Esau he had to face another Antagonist. The story that follows is a very strange one. There are some interesting primitive features in it. Like Hamlet's ghost, Jacob's mysterious antagonist had to depart before the day broke. The touch on Jacob's thigh was recognized by the Old Testament writer as the reason for a Hebrew taboo which forbade the eating of the sciatic muscle of animals. Such details raise interesting questions about the original form and meaning of this old story but they do not affect the Biblical meaning. In its present form the story is clearly a symbolical description of a religious experience. Jacob had reached a second, and more critical, turning-point in the development of his character.

The meaning of the story comes out very clearly in the conversation which marks its climax. True to his nature Jacob sought to win a blessing from his spiritual antagonist. Jacob was always quick to seek advantage for himself. But he was faced this time with a searching question: 'What is thy name?' When we remember the close connection between the name and the nature in Biblical tradition this question becomes full of meaning. Jacob was being compelled to acknowledge what kind of person he really was. Self-knowledge is a painful experience but it is a necessary condition of all growth in character. Jacob, during his lonely vigil, was conscious once again, as he had been at Bethel twenty years before, that his dearest hopes were threatened. At Bethel he had received the assurance that God would be with him in all his journeyings. He had been ready to make a bargain with God and God seemed to have given him all he wanted. Now he tried to win a blessing from God again but this time it was not so easy. The danger from which he sought deliverance was the fruit of his own deceitful nature. His real enemy was within. Before he could receive any blessing he must face, before God, the facts of his own nature.

'I am Jacob', he said. And in these words he acknowledged the weakness which his name described. He had prided himself on his great achievements in Haran. He had been thinking of himself as a man of great wealth and power and he had been ready to patronize his elder brother. But now he was forced to acknowledge his own true nature. The long night of spiritual wrestling ended in humble acknowledgement of the bitter truth. And this simple confession of his weakness proved the first step towards new strength. His name was changed to Israel as evidence of his spiritual victory.

Jacob meets Esau (Gen. xxxiii.)

When Jacob met Esau he learned that his fears had been needless. Esau had had no hostile intentions. His impulsive nature responded to present circumstances, as it always had done. He had never concerned himself much about future possibilities, and he bore no grudge against his brother because of past events. His welcome was generous and sincere. He was quick to offer the protection of his bodyguard but Jacob, still hesitant and fearful, deemed it wiser that they should part. And so Jacob returned in safety to the land of his fathers and he built an altar at Shechem.

CHAPTER 4

JOSEPH, AND HIS BROTHERS

Is Joseph a historical figure?
The story of Joseph differs, in several ways, from the stories of Abraham, Isaac and Jacob. In the first place, it is a single continuous story and not just a collection of loosely connected episodes. A definite plot is unfolded. We watch the interplay of character and circumstances and we follow the changing fortunes of the central character. It is a romantic story of a spoiled child who suffers humiliation and rises later to a position of great power and influence. It is also a parable of human life. It sets before us in story form, some of the most familiar teaching of the Bible about human character and conduct.

There is an important difference, too, in the religious outlook of these characters. Joseph has no visions or striking religious experiences. Even his dreams have no direct religious meaning. There are no incidents associated with shrines or sacred places. The story of Joseph is a typical oriental tale in which God is hardly mentioned. Nevertheless the writer is clearly conscious of the overruling providence of God influencing the course of events. Joseph himself expresses that view of his experiences in his reassuring words to his brothers: 'But as for you, ye thought evil against me; but God meant it unto good, to bring to pass, as it is this day, to save much people alive. Now therefore fear ye not : I will nourish you and your little ones". (Gen. i. 20f.)

The continuous, and closely woven, nature of the story raises an interesting question. The earlier stories look like fragments of historical tradition. They seem to preserve the memory of people, places and events prominent in early Hebrew traditions. But the story of Joseph and his brothers is different. It is a self-contained account of a family situation. The sons of Israel, in the story, all play individual parts which seem to have no connection with the early fortunes of the Israelite tribes which are named after them. The only exception to this statement helps to emphasize its general truth. In chapter xxxviii there is a detached episode in which we find Judah separated from his brothers and settled in the south of Canaan. This does not harmonize with the rest of the story and it looks like a bit of early tradition about the tribe of Judah. We know that that tribe inhabited the south of Canaan and there are reasons for believing that it was never enslaved in Egypt. What view then should we take of this story of Joseph and his brothers? Is it based on actual historical happenings? Did the ancestors of the Jewish people all spend a prolonged period in Egypt? Did one of their number rise to a position of great power and influence at the court of Egypt?

The Semitic rulers of Egypt
The evidence available does not allow us to give a definite answer to these questions. We know that Egypt was ruled from about 1700 to 1570 B.C. by invaders called the Hyksos and it is believed that the Hyksos were mostly of Semitic race. In such circumstances a Hebrew family might be favourably received in Egypt and the overthrow of the Hyksos rulers might correspond to the rise of a 'new king over Egypt which knew not Joseph' (Exod. i. 8). The dates fit reasonably well and the circumstances seem to provide an appropriate historical setting for the Biblical narrative.

Evidence from the Bible
On the other hand there are difficulties and inconsistencies in the Bible record itself. The detached episode about Judah, referred to above, seems to suggest that the tribe of Judah had traditional associations with the south of Canaan and may never have entered Egypt. Other Biblical evidence strengthens the view that only some of the early Hebrews were in Egypt. We are told twice that there were seventy persons in the company who settled in Goshen (Gen. xlvi. 27; Exod. i. 5) yet the earlier stories of Abraham and Isaac give the impression of a large number of dependants. When we look at the last

chapter of Joshua we find an account of a great gathering of the Israelite tribes being held at Shechem. There is no record of Shechem being captured by the Hebrew invaders who entered Canaan with Joshua but the stories of Jacob include an account of its conquest by his two sons Levi and Simeon (Gen xxxiv.). And the purpose of the gathering at Shechem, according to the Bible story, was to hear a speech from Joshua in which he summoned all the assembled tribes to make a choice of religious loyalties and declared that he and his house would worship the LORD who had brought them out of the land of Egypt.

Two distinct traditions
When all the evidence is examined it seems clear that there were two main groups of early Hebrew tradition. One group preserved the memory of migrations from the Tigris-Euphrates valley and a settlement in Canaan. Abraham, Isaac and Jacob belong to that group of traditions. Abraham came from Haran. Isaac and Jacob each found a wife in the ancestral home. The second group of traditions told of a period of slavery in Egypt and of a great deliverance. The stories of Moses and the Exodus belong to that tradition. This deliverance from Egypt became the foundation fact in the religious faith of all the tribes of Israel although the actual experience may have been confined to those few tribes which had lived for a while as slaves in Egypt. The account of Joshua's challenge to the tribes assembled at Shechem helps to strengthen that view.

Family relationships in an oriental household (Gen. xxxvii. 1–11)
The tradition of a sojourn in Egypt is certainly inseparable from the Biblical record even if the story of Joseph and his brothers does not have a firm foundation in historical fact. The writer may have used genuine traditions about a Hebrew who held high office at the Egyptian court or he may have used a well-known popular tale. We cannot be certain. He has certainly created a matchless and romantic story which

provides a link between the two groups of early traditions and accounts for the presence of Israelite ancestors in Egypt.

The whole story offers a fascinating study of human behaviour. The setting is a typical oriental household. Jacob (or Israel) was the father. Rachel was Jacob's favourite wife, for whom he had served fourteen years in Haran. She had only two sons, Joseph and Benjamin. Rachel's elder sister Leah had six sons and a daughter. There were also four other sons, two born to each of two concubines. There were thus four mothers in one household, each likely to be jealous of the other's relationship with Jacob and each passionately concerned for the rights and privileges of her own children. The possibilities of family trouble are obvious.

The sin of Jacob

It was natural that Jacob should have tender feelings towards Rachel's first-born child. The same feeling is shown towards Benjamin, who was also Rachel's child, in the latter part of the story. But Jacob allowed these tender feelings to influence his attitude as a father. Joseph became his father's favourite child. Jacob's tender feelings were natural. His favouritism was sinful.

The sin of Joseph

Joseph's dreams have much to tell us about his inner thoughts and feelings. The Bible story suggests that the dreams were prophetic of Joseph's future greatness. No doubt they were. A man's dreams may tell us a great deal about his nature and its possibilities. But Joseph's dreams may also throw some light on his early experiences in that oriental household. Dreams often compensate, we are told, for the realities of waking life. A hungry man may dream of food. A poor man may dream of wealth. Joseph dreamed of power. His brothers, and even his father and mother, were acknowledging him, in his dreams, as their superior. Did these dreams, perhaps, compensate for experiences in waking life? He was the youngest in a large family. Had he felt acutely conscious of his helpless inferiority, as a small child among older brothers? Had he been the target of early jealousy and resentment, as the child of Jacob's favourite wife? If that were so we can understand that Jacob's feelings for Joseph would help to strengthen his position in the household and would provide the sense of security which he might otherwise have lacked.

It was natural that Joseph should appreciate his father's affection. If he had inner feelings of inferiority and insecurity he would cling more strongly to every evidence of his father's appreciation and protection. But Joseph allowed these feelings, natural enough in the circumstances, to give birth to an attitude of arrogant vanity. It is evident from the story that there was more than a hint of arrogance in his manner of describing his dreams. Even his father rebuked him. And his use of the 'coat of many colours' speaks plainly. The English phrase is misleading. The original Hebrew means literally 'a tunic of palms' and it implies a long sleeved garment reaching down to the palms of the hands and the soles of the feet. It was a garment for festive occasions and it was certainly not appropriate for a long journey. Yet it was this garment in which Joseph set out to find his brothers. Joseph's appreciation of his father's special affection was natural. His arrogant vanity was sinful.

The sin of the brothers

It was natural that Joseph's brothers should resent Jacob's favouritism towards his young son. It was not surprising that Joseph's dreams should irritate them and his arrogance provoke them. But they nursed their resentment and allowed it to grow into dangerous envy and hatred. And in doing so, they were acting sinfully.

The varied relationships in this human family stand in strong contrast to Biblical teaching about God, the Heavenly Father, and His purpose for the lives of His children. Where love is perfect there are no favourite children. All are treated alike. God 'maketh His sun to rise on the evil and on the good and sendeth rain on the just and on the unjust' (Matt. v. 45). And the love which Christ awakens in His followers, 'Knows no jealousy . . . gives itself no airs, is never rude, never selfish, never irritated, never resentful' (1 Cor. xiii. 4–5: Moffatt translation).

The fruit of sin (Gen. xxxvii. 12–36)

When God's laws are ignored disaster is inevitable. This truth, too, is illustrated in the story. Jacob, Joseph and the ten brothers had all failed to follow God's perfect law of love. In the early part of the story they behaved as ordinary men and women constantly behave. The development of the story shows what serious consequences may spring from such everyday behaviour. Men were quick to use the knife in those days. Modern society controls the murderous impulse but hard feelings still bear bitter fruit in family life. Even in modern times war has been the ultimate method of settling disputes between nations and war has its roots in men's failure to live together as brethren, acknowledging the love of their common Heavenly Father.

Joseph's journey to Dothan gave his brothers an opportunity for action. The sight of his 'coat of many colours' may have acted as a spark to their explosive feelings and 'they conspired against him to slay him'. The development of the plot is not very clear at this point and it is evident that two different versions of the story have been combined. In one, Reuben figures in a more favourable light. He persuades his brothers to cast Joseph into a pit and leave him to die, thus avoiding bloodshed. He returns alone to the pit to deliver him but finds it empty, for passing Midianites had carried Joseph off with them to Egypt. In the other version Judah persuades his brothers to avoid bloodshed by selling Joseph to a company of Ishmaelites who are travelling to Egypt. The differences are unimportant. The important fact is that Joseph is carried off to be sold into slavery in Egypt while the brothers go home and report his death to their father Jacob.

The change in Joseph (Gen. xl.–xli.)

Joseph's early experiences in Egypt might have made him hard and bitter. He had been the spoiled favourite of his father in a wealthy household and he found himself carried off to be sold in an Egyptian slave-market. He was bought for service in Pharaoh's household and he prospered there, but he was falsely accused and he was cast into prison. He won the favour of the prison governor and interpreted the dreams of two fellow-prisoners but he learned what human ingratitude can mean and he had to bear the pain of disappointed hopes for two whole years. Then came a dramatic change in his fortunes. Joseph was summoned to Pharaoh's court to interpret a royal dream and, in a short time, he found himself with supreme power in the land under Pharaoh himself. The early humiliation and suffering combined with this sudden elevation to power and influence were a severe test of Joseph's character. If he had yielded to natural impulses Joseph's early vanity might have grown beyond all bounds and he might have seized eagerly on the opportunity to avenge himself on his brothers. But Joseph was a changed man.

The change in the brothers (Gen. xlii.–xliii.)

The scenes between Joseph and his brothers are full of human interest. Joseph recognized his brothers but they did not know him. His behaviour towards them was obviously intended to test them. Were they still the same untrustworthy characters, moved by self-interest and careless of their father's feelings? Would they be ready to abandon Benjamin to an uncertain fate as they had abandoned Joseph? There was no reason to expect anything else. They had harboured a guilty secret through twenty years and that does not often have a good effect on human character. If Joseph's brothers had followed their natural human impulses during these years there might well have been further tragedies in the family situation. But they, too, were changed men.

The conversation in Canaan between Jacob and his sons is most revealing. The change revealed in the brothers is most striking. Reuben and Judah again took the initiative. Each in turn volunteered to accept responsibility for Benjamin's safety. The father's feelings are poignantly expressed in his words and attitude. Only the compulsion of necessity made him agree to risk the loss of Rachel's remaining child. But

necessity did prevail and the brothers set out again for Egypt.
  Joseph's feelings almost betrayed him when he saw his brother Benjamin again. The child he had remembered was now grown into manhood. But he controlled himself. The test was not yet complete. As they sat at meat, however, Joseph made sure that his own mother's child was given generous portions of the best dishes. Then he made his plans. The brothers were sent on their homeward journey with their sacks filled, but Joseph's own silver cup was placed in Benjamin's sack.

Joseph and his brothers are reconciled (Gen. xliv.–xlv.)
  And now we reach the climax of the story. Messengers were sent after the brothers to accuse them of theft. Confident of innocence the brothers protested that death for the guilty party and slavery for the others would be a fitting punishment for such a gross breach of hospitality and trust. The sacks were opened and the cup was found. In great distress the brothers returned together and came before Joseph. When he saw them together Joseph must have realized that his test had already been answered. The brothers were not deserting Benjamin in his danger. But Joseph was not yet satisfied. He dismissed the suggestion that any but Benjamin should suffer punishment. Let Benjamin remain as a slave and the others might go free.
  Judah's eloquent plea for Benjamin is one of the most moving passages in the Old Testament. He described in vivid words the pathetic circumstances in which they had taken leave of their old father. He told of the earlier bereavement and of his certainty that the loss of Benjamin would cause his father's death. In Judah's closing words Joseph received convincing evidence of the change in his brothers for Judah offered himself as a slave in place of Benjamin: 'For how shall I go up to my father and the lad be not with me? lest I see the evil that shall come upon my father?' Joseph's feelings could stand no more. Sending his servants away he made himself known to his brothers and comforted them in their guilty consternation and dismay.

Joseph's father and brothers settle in Goshen (Gen. xlvi. 28-34; xlvii.1-12, 29-31)

It is a story of guilt and forgiveness, of estrangement and reconciliation and of the overruling providence of God. It shows how wrong human relationships can lead to disaster but it shows, too, that human character and conduct are not determined by circumstances. In the beginning of the story we see how circumstances betrayed Jacob, Joseph and the ten brothers into wrong attitudes and actions. They allowed natural impulses to control their conduct. And disaster followed. But the later part of the story shows how Joseph and his brothers rose triumphantly above the influence of circumstances. They responded to the influences of divine grace, as the theologian would put it. Reconciliation followed and the disaster itself became a means by which life was preserved (cf. Gen. xlv. 5, 7). Jacob himself was brought to Egypt to see, again, his long lost child. Pharaoh received Joseph's relatives most graciously and provided for them most generously. They were given the fertile land of Goshen, on the eastern frontier of Egypt, for their flocks and herds. There they settled and there Jacob died. But, on his deathbed, Jacob exacted a promise from Joseph that his bones should be buried in the home land of Canaan.

PART II

GOD AND MAN
IN THE MAKING OF A NATION

CHAPTER 5

MOSES, THE PROPHETIC LEADER AND LAWGIVER

The Exodus Stories: What really happened?
The book of Exodus tells us of the events which gave birth to the religious faith of the Hebrews and it shows us how a body of slaves began to grow into a nation. In this book we are in direct touch with historical events and experiences. It may be difficult to prove that Abraham, Jacob or Joseph were real figures of history. It may be quite certain that many of the religious ideas which we meet in the book of Genesis are those of the writer rather than of the individuals about whom he is writing. But it would be difficult to deny that Moses ever lived or to claim that the escape of the Israelites from Egypt never happened. The influence of Moses and the events in which he played a leading part have left an indelible mark on the national and religious life of the Jewish people throughout their whole history.

The book of Exodus, however, is not a history book. It does not give us an accurate account of historical happenings, as they might have been described by a contemporary reporter. The purpose of the writers was quite different. They were not trying to preserve a detailed record of actual happenings. They were much more concerned about the religious *meaning* of the events. The book of Exodus is, therefore, much more like a creed, a triumphant assertion of religious belief, than a sober record of factual history. Nevertheless the creed, the religious belief, that is professed in it is a belief about the meaning of *actual historical events*.

The book that we read in our Bible was not written until long after the events about which it tells. The memory of these events would probably be preserved in earliest times through a recital of them as part of a religious service. Even today the story of the Exodus is retold every year as part of the Jewish

MOSES, THE PROPHETIC LEADER AND LAWGIVER 35

religious festival of the Passover. From the beginning, therefore, the events would be coloured by the poetic imagery of eastern religious devotion. When the Israelites entered Canaan more than one version of this story would be preserved in different parts of the country. There is evidence that different versions have been combined in the written book and it is quite clear that our book of Exodus, like most books of the Old Testament, was the work of an editor, or editors, using earlier written material.

Is it possible for us to get behind the written record, as we have it, and discover what the actual events may have been? Can we tell how the Israelites actually got across the 'Red Sea'? Was Mt Sinai a volcanic mountain? Did a column of smoke from such a mountain, lit by volcanic flames at night, give rise to the tradition of the pillar of fire and smoke which guided the Israelites? It is certainly true that the Jordan valley is part of a great geological fault which extends southwards by the Gulf of Akaba and the Red Sea into north-east Africa and this region has been liable to earthquake and volcanic disturbance. It is also true that the stories of the plagues of Egypt, the crossing of the 'Red Sea' and the Jordan, the pillar of cloud and fire, the smoke and fire at Mt Sinai, the collapse of the city walls at Jericho, could all be explained by earthquake or volcanic action. But we cannot be certain regarding the actual happenings. All we know quite certainly is that the ancestors of the Jewish people escaped from Egypt in circumstances which left a profound impression on them and convinced them of the truth of Moses' teaching.

When did the Exodus take place? (Exod. i. 8–14)

Many attempts have been made to link the story of Moses with established facts of Egyptian history. We know that Thutmose III, who died about 1436 B.C., carried out many building schemes and that he employed Semitic captives in such work. A tomb has been found in Upper Egypt which shows pictures of them at work and an inscription describing the picture quotes words of the taskmaster: 'The rod is in my hand: be not idle'. On the other hand there is no evidence of any such building in the Nile Delta at that time and it is there that the Bible places the Israelites.

The opening chapter of Exodus tells us that the Israelites built 'store-cities, Pithom and Raamses' for Pharaoh. Some archaeologists claim to have identified the ruins of these two cities. They say that Raamses was a royal residence in the Delta which was extended and improved by Raamses II (c. 1301–1234 B.C.) and that Pithom was also built, or rebuilt, by him. This would suggest that Moses and the Exodus belonged to this later period.

No evidence has been found in Egyptian records which tells of the events of the Exodus. This is not surprising. The escape of a company of Semitic slaves is hardly likely to have made a lasting impression on Egyptian memories, even though it was accompanied by severe and unusual natural disasters. Further evidence may yet enable us to date these events with greater accuracy and to relate them more closely to Egyptian history. Meantime we must be content to recognize that the Biblical story is quite compatible with the known facts and to acknowledge that we cannot be certain about the exact date.

What do we know about Moses? (Exod. ii.)

The Jewish historian Josephus (c. A.D. 37–100) has preserved some traditions about Moses which do not appear in the Old Testament. He tells us that Moses served as a general in the Egyptian army in an expedition against the Ethiopians and that he married an Ethiopian princess (cf. Num. xii. 1). A number of attempts have also been made to fill out our knowledge of Moses by following up various possible clues in the text of the Bible. Some years ago Sigmund Freud, the famous psychologist, developed an elaborate and ingenious theory in *Moses and Monotheism*. Such speculation may be interesting but it is not very illuminating. The groundwork of fact cannot support such an elaborate structure of theory.

It is much more useful, for our purpose, to examine carefully the traditions about Moses' childhood and early manhood which have been preserved in the Bible. These are likely to give us a picture of the man as he was remembered in the religious traditions of his own people. They do, in fact, give us some significant information about him. They tell us that he was born of Hebrew parents and nurtured by his mother but that he was adopted into the Egyptian royal family and 'instructed in all the wisdom of the Egyptians' (Acts vii. 22). Three incidents are recorded which reveal the young man, as he was remembered in the traditions of his people. Each one shows an impetuous, hot-blooded man with a passion for fair-play. He is revolted at the sight of the Egyptian taskmasters illtreating his fellow-countrymen and he kills one. He intervenes in a dispute between two Hebrews. He comes to the aid of some woman at a well in Midian. Moses seems to have been unable to see injustice done without springing to the defence of the injured party.

This was the man who felt God's call to deliver the Israelite slaves from Egypt. He was living in Midian at the time. He had had to flee from Egypt because he had slain an Egyptian. One of the young women at the well had become his wife, and he had settled in Midian in the household of Jethro, his father-in-law. Following the traditional occupation of his Hebrew ancestors he was looking after Jethro's sheep. There would be long hours when he was alone with the sheep and, at such times, his thoughts must often have turned back on his experiences in Egypt. He would surely brood over the sufferings of his people at the hand of Pharaoh. God speaks to men continually but few are able to hear and fewer still are willing to respond. Moses heard God speak because he was already concerned about the sufferings of his fellows.

Moses at Mount Horeb (Exod. iii. 1–12)

The story of Moses' experience on Mount Horeb is the record of a man's encounter with God. It is, therefore, on Moses and not on the bush that our attention should be fixed. We cannot tell now what striking and unusual sight may have arrested Moses' attention. The circumstances could only have been described by Moses himself and such a story would naturally have a prominent place, from the beginning, in the account of the great events by which the Israelites were delivered from slavery. It is likely that eastern symbolism has affected the form of the story which has come down to us. We know that fire was a frequent symbol for the presence of God (cf. Exod. xix. 18; Ezek. i. 27; viii. 2; 1 Kings xviii. 24; 2 Chron. vii. 1). The 'flame of fire' and the bush that 'burned with fire' may therefore be symbolical ways of saying that Moses knew that God was near. We cannot be sure what it was that Moses really saw but it is the inner meaning of the experience which really matters. There is no reason to doubt that that meaning has been faithfully preserved.

Five aspects of Moses' experience can be distinguished in the story. There is, first, the disturbing sense of God's presence. Horeb is called 'the mountain of God'. It was already a 'holy place' and Moses may have known of its sacred associations for the people dwelling in Midian. But to Moses it was the God of his fathers, the God of whom his mother had taught him, of whose presence he was now aware (vv. 5f.). The second aspect of his experience is the realization that God cares about the suffering of the Hebrew slaves in Egypt. Here is a new revelation of God's nature. Moses realizes that his own burning passion for justice is the very voice of God Himself. The God of his fathers is a God of justice (vv. 7f.). Awareness of this truth is followed, or accompanied, by a deep conviction that God would have him go back to Egypt and lead his people out of slavery (v.10). Such a task overwhelms him with a sense of inadequacy (v. 11) and there follows the assurance that God Himself will be with him and the promise that he will be enabled to bring the Israelites to this very mountain to give thanks for their deliverance.

These features in Moses' experience are typical of every profound experience of God. Every such experience includes an unusually strong awareness of the presence of God. There is generally some aspect of the divine nature which comes home to the individual more clearly and convincingly than ever before. When that happens there must be some response in action. The individual knows that he must do something about it. Such knowledge naturally awakens a feeling of personal

MOSES, THE PROPHETIC LEADER AND LAWGIVER

weakness but the experience carries with it the assurance of divine help. In those moments when men commit themselves, without reserve, to the will of God they know that no power in the universe can overwhelm them. (cf. Ps. xlvi).

The meaning of the Divine Name (Exod. iv. 13-15)

Verses 13-15 give us a rather puzzling account of the name by which Moses is to speak of God to the Israelites: 'Thus shalt thou say unto the children of Israel, The LORD God of your fathers, the God of Abraham, the God of Isaac, and the God of Jacob hath sent me unto you... this is my name for ever'. The Hebrew word יהוה which is printed as LORD in the Old Testament was probably originally pronounced as Yahweh and it is often printed in that way now (or Jahweh) in books about the Old Testament. In the early centuries of Hebrew writing the vowels were omitted and only the consonants were written. By the time a system of vowel signs began to be used (after A.D. 500) the Jews regarded the name of God as much too sacred to be pronounced. For that reason the sacred name was, and is, never written, or printed, with the vowels which would give its true pronunciation. The vowels of the Hebrew word for LORD are inserted instead. Our word Jehovah comes from an attempt to pronounce this combination of consonants and vowels. When a passage containing the sacred name is read in the synagogue, however, the reader substitutes the word LORD and so our English translations use the word but print it in capital letters to show that it stands for the sacred name of God.

This passage shows us what the word Jahweh meant to the Old Testament writers. They regarded it as the third person singular of the verb *to be*. Hebrew verbs have only two tenses. The imperfect tense is the tense of uncompleted action and the perfect tense is the tense of completed action. Jahweh is in the imperfect tense and it may, therefore, be translated 'He who is' or 'He who will be'. The verb is used in the first person in v. 14 and the A.V. translates it as if it were the present tense: 'I am that I am'. Use of the present tense, however, makes the meaning rather abstract and early Hebrew thought was very seldom abstract. We should, therefore, translate the words in v. 14 as 'I will be what I will be' and take the sacred name as meaning 'He will be'. In course of time the word simply became the name by which the Israelites knew and worshipped God but it is interesting to realize that they used to think of it in this way. In this passage the writer is apparently suggesting that God made Himself known to Moses as one who would be known more fully to His people as they experienced his saving presence in their history.

This is one of the passages which helps to make it clear that the religious faith of the Old Testament began with the experience of deliverance from Egypt. The God of Israel was 'the LORD (i.e. Jahweh) our God . . . that brought us up and our fathers out of the land of Egypt, from the house of bondage' (Joshua xxiv. 17). It seems strange to read in Gen. iv. 25 that men began 'to call upon the name of the LORD' in the days of Seth, the son of Adam. At first sight that statement seems to contradict the passage in Exodus which we have been examining. In reality it shows that the Old Testament writers were quite sure that the LORD, the God of Israel, had been known from the beginning although his real nature only began to be fully disclosed in the deliverance of the Israelites from slavery (cf. also Exod. vi. 2f.).

Moses and Aaron approach Pharaoh (Exod. iv. 1–7; v.)

The name of Aaron was remembered in Israelite tradition as one who had been associated with Moses in the events of the Exodus. In later centuries the Levites, an inferior order in the priesthood, traced their descent to Aaron, the brother of Moses, who was given the task of assisting him in his approach to Pharaoh. Chapter 4 shows how hesitant Moses was to undertake the formidable task which faced him and tells of God's promise that Aaron would assist him. The story of the signs given to Moses describe that hesitation in a picturesque way and need not be regarded as an account of an historical incident.

In Chapter 5 we are introduced to a contrast which is repeated again and again in the pages of the Old Testament.

The chapter tells of the first approach to Pharaoh and its results. Moses and Aaron sought permission for the Israelites to make a pilgrimage into the desert in order to sacrifice to the LORD. Pharaoh refused the request and ordered his taskmasters to treat the Hebrew slaves with greater severity. When that happened the Israelites at once blamed Moses and Aaron for mishandling the situation and Moses, on his part, brought their troubles to God. Moses was back in Egypt because of his experience at Mt Horeb. In all his actions he was conscious of fulfilling a divine command and in every situation he turned to God, in prayer, for guidance and help. The Israelites, however, had been persuaded by Moses to follow his leadership. Their faith in the LORD was not based on personal experience and it did not stand the test of adversity.

The Origin of the Passover (Exod. xii. 1-36)

The final escape from Egypt is inseparably associated in Jewish tradition with the feast of the Passover. In Exod. xii. 21, however, 'the Passover' is named, without explanation, as if it were already familiar. Students of the Old Testament believe that the origin of it goes back much further than the days of Moses. It seems to be associated with the sacrifice of first-born animals (and possibly originally of first-born sons) in primitive nomadic life. The feast of unleavened bread, on the other hand (Exod. xii. 17) was one of three annual agricultural feasts which the Israelites probably took over from the Canaanites when they settled in Canaan. The two festivals became blended into one and associated with the escape from Egypt.

How did this association arise? It seems reasonable to suppose that it was a 'passover' celebration of which Moses spoke in the Exodus story when he asked Pharaoh's permission for the Israelites to go and sacrifice in the desert. It was obviously remembered in Jewish tradition that the immediate reason for Pharaoh's consent to their departure was a devastating pestilence which struck the Egyptians killing, perhaps, Pharaoh's own eldest son. The Israelites in the land of Goshen might well have escaped and their immunity would be associated ever afterwards with the other striking events of their deliverance. And these events were probably connected, as we have seen, with a passover celebration planned by Moses. New meaning would thus be read into ancient customs and the traditional associations of the passover festival would be gradually established.

The twelfth chapter of Exodus is full of religious teaching but it need not be regarded as a detailed account of actual happenings at the time of the Israelite escape from Egypt. It is a chapter in which the Old Testament writers trace the connection between that great event and the religious beliefs and customs of their own age. The blood of the passover lamb came to be regarded as the symbol which protected the Israelite households from the pestilence which struck the Egyptians. The passover sacrifice also came to be associated with the idea of atonement for sin, and deliverance from sin. This thought is developed in the New Testament where Paul speaks of 'Christ our passover . . . sacrificed for us' (1 Cor. v. 7). The blood of the passover lamb smeared on the doorposts of the Israelites, according to their tradition, delivered them from destruction by the pestilence. In Paul's thought that blood becomes a symbol of the sacrificial death of Christ, by which men are delivered from the destructive power of sin.

The pillar of cloud and fire (Exod. xiii. 17–22)

The direct route from Egypt to Canaan lay by the sea coast but Hebrew tradition spoke of a long period of wandering in the desert area to the south of Canaan. Why did the Israelites not go by the direct route? Such a question would naturally occur to the Old Testament writers and an explanation is offered in Exod. xiii. 17f. In the days when the story was being written down the Philistines dwelt on the sea coasts of Canaan and were a continual menace to the Israelites. Here was an obvious explanation. The Israelites had lived as slaves in Egypt and were quite unfit to fight their way through territory occupied by so formidable a foe. And so the editor inserted his comment.

These Old Testament writers always bore faithful witness

to the religious facts although they sometimes went astray in their historical explanations. The Philistines had not yet settled in Palestine when the Israelites left Egypt so they could not have offered any opposition to an Israelite advance by the coast. On this historical point the Old Testament editor was mistaken. But he pointed unerringly to the religious reality. He went astray when he tried to interpret the historical reasons for the route taken by the escaping Israelites but he preserved faithfully and recorded unerringly the religious experience of his people in these far-off days. They had known beyond any possibility of doubt that it was God himself who was leading them.

Israelite tradition told of a pillar of cloud and of fire which guided them continually. That tradition may have had its origin in the fact that Mt Sinai was a volcanic mountain. The mountain has commonly been identified with the Jebel Musa in the south of the Sinai peninsula but some writers believe that it lay on the east side of the Gulf of Akaba where there is evidence of volcanic action in the past. The description in Exod. xix. 16, 18 certainly suggests volcanic activity. It would have been a most awe-inspiring experience for Moses and the Israelites to see a great pillar of smoke apparently beckoning them towards the very mountain where Moses himself had met God (Sinai and Horeb are two alternative names for the same mountain; cf. Exod. iii. 1; xix. 20 and Deut. v. 2). But like the Old Testament historian we may go astray when we seek historical explanations. We cannot be sure that this attractive suggestion points to the true origin of the tradition. Of one thing, however, there can be no doubt. This people knew that they had been led by God throughout all their wanderings

It might be truer to say that Moses possessed this sublime religious confidence, for it is obvious from the Old Testament record that the people wavered continually between triumphant trust and faithless fear. The story of the 'Red Sea' crossing illustrates again the contrast between the confidence of Moses and the fears of the Israelites. When it seemed clear that they were caught between the chariots of the Egyptians and the waters of the 'Red Sea' the Israelites again turned on Moses with bitter reproaches. In the same situation Moses had no doubts or hesitations. He had committed himself to God for the fulfilment of His purposes and the very voice of God seemed to ring in his ears: 'Speak unto the children of Israel, that they go forward'.

The Red Sea crossing (Exod. xiv.)

There is no certainty about the geographical setting of the 'Red Sea' crossing. One fact is clear. The Israelites did not cross the broad stretch of water which we know as the Red Sea. The Hebrew text speaks of the *Yam Sūph* or 'sea of reeds' and the A.V. translation is most misleading. It is based on the Greek and Latin versions of the text. The term *Yam Sūph* is used in 1 Kings ix: 26 to describe the northern end of the Gulf of Akaba and some writers suggest that it was there that the crossing took place. They would also locate Mt Sinai (or Horeb) in that same area, on the east side of the Gulf, where some extinct volcanoes are to be found. On the other hand the term *Yam Sūph* would describe appropriately the swampy area north of the Gulf of Suez where the Suez Canal now lies and it is more commonly believed that the escape took place at that point. Mt Sinai would then be located at the traditional site to the south of the Sinai peninsula.

The account of the actual crossing provides an interesting illustration of the Old Testament editors' habit of combining earlier written traditions about the same event. Any careful reader of Exod. xiv. 21–31 must be conscious of repetition and of the presence of phrases offering alternative explanations of the event. V. 21 begins and ends with clauses which point to a miraculous dividing of the waters when Moses raised his rod over the sea. In the middle of the verse we find a picture of an event caused by a strong east wind. Students of the Hebrew text have separated out from the passage two distinct and complete accounts which differ in just that way. One describes a 'natural' event which enabled the Israelites to escape while the chariots of the Egyptians stuck in the soft mud (in v. 25 we should read 'bound' for 'took off') and were

MOSES, THE PROPHETIC LEADER AND LAWGIVER 45

caught by the returning waters. The other describes a 'miraculous' event in which the raising of Moses' rod controls the movement of the waters.

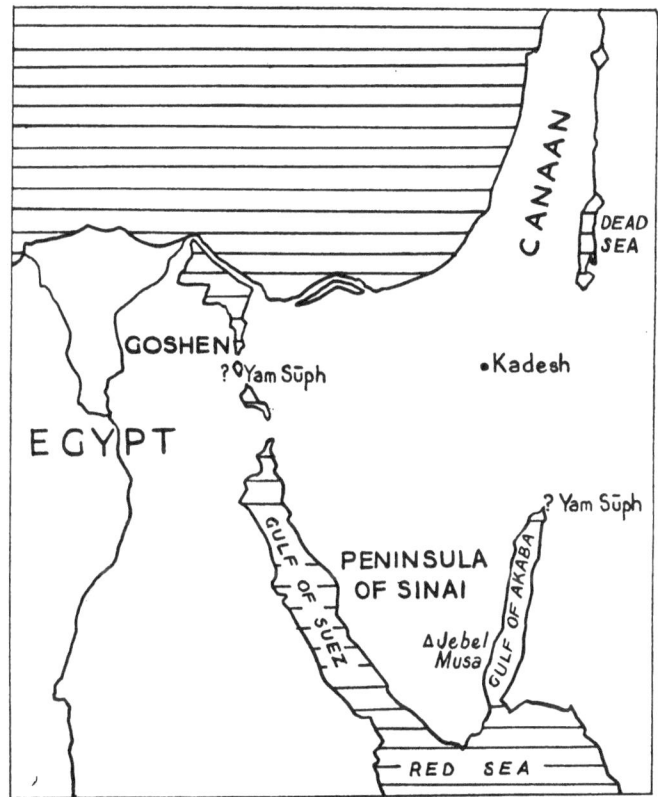

From Egypt to Canaan

It seems strange to us that editors should use earlier records in this way but we have convincing evidence that that used to be done. We still have parts of a second century life of Christ which was prepared in just that way. The writer (Tatian) had used the four gospels and had made a single consecutive account by piecing together passages taken from them. This practice certainly helps to explain many passages in the Old Testament where more than one account of the incident is obviously contained within the text of the Old Testament passage.

The certainty of religious faith

It is important that we should notice, however, that both accounts of the escape at the Red Sea agree in the ultimate explanation which they give. One tradition describes the Israelite escape in more dramatic terms than the other but both are equally certain that it was a divine deliverance. Either tradition might have originated in events which we could explain today in 'natural' terms. The more dramatic one suggests some cataclysmic movements of land and water caused by earthquake. The other suggests special conditions of wind and tide. To the Old Testament writers such differences were comparatively unimportant. When all had seemed lost Moses had bade the people go forward, committing themselves in trust to God. They had done so and God had delivered them. A modern unbeliever might say that an unusual, but not unnatural, happening had taken place, by coincidence, at the very moment when the Israelites were able to profit by it. Moses and the Israelites saw in that 'coincidence' a miraculous divine deliverance. That was the certainty of historical experience and religious conviction on which the whole faith of the Old Testament was built.

That is the kind of certainty on which all Biblical faith is built. It does not really matter whether or not we can find a scientific explanation of the Exodus events. Christian conviction does not rest on some infallible signs which cannot be explained or denied. Nor does it rest on wonder stories which cannot stand the test of critical examination. The Christian commits himself in trust to life, believing that the ultimate power in the universe is a spiritual being whose nature can be seen in Jesus Christ. As he does so he finds that experience confirms his belief. He is conscious of providential guidance and succour in events which the non-Christian might explain in 'natural' terms.

The Christian and the non-Christian live in the same universe. And the world of the Old Testament is not different from our world. Its laws are the same today as they were in the days of Moses, although our partial understanding of these laws is vastly greater than the Israelites possessed. The real difference between the Christian and the non-Christian, between the writers of the Bible and a modern unbeliever, lies in their ultimate attitude to the universe. The one acknowledges that he did not make himself and he commits himself in trust to God 'as unto a faithful creator' (1 Peter iv. 19). The other either refuses to admit his dependence or refuses to trust his creator. Because of that difference the one finds God in the universe and the other is blind to his presence.

Life in the desert

The Biblical record tells that the Israelites spent a period of forty years wandering in the desert before they entered the promised land. We are only given fragmentary glimpses of the events of that period and it is not possible to form a clear picture of the order of these events, or of their geographical location. It is generally agreed, as we have seen, that Horeb and Sinai are different names for the same mountain. The book of Exodus tells us that Moses gave the Israelites the ten commandments and led them into covenant with God at Mt Sinai (Exod. xx. & xxiv.), while Deuteronomy places the same events at Mt Horeb (Deut. v). But the references to Sinai and to Horeb seem to place them, respectively, on the west and on the east side of the Gulf of Akaba. It is obvious that the position, as well as the name, of the sacred mountain differed in the different traditions.

Careful study of the Old Testament accounts of this period brings two places into prominence. One is the sacred mountain, Sinai or Horeb. The other is Kadesh, which is generally identified with a spring called 'Ain Qedeis. This spring lies about sixty miles in a south-westerly direction from the southern end of the Dead Sea. There are three springs in the area and the Israelites may have used these springs as a base to which they returned regularly to water their flocks. It seems possible that they planned to enter Canaan from the south but were defeated and discouraged in an early attempt. They may then have lived in the desert, with Kadesh as their centre, until a new and more courageous generation had grown up to replace those who had been slaves in Egypt.

It is clear, at least, that this desert period must have been a most important stage in Israel's national and religious history. The religious faith of Israel must have begun as the religious faith of Moses. It was he who had the memorable experience at Mt Horeb which sent him back to Egypt. It was he who led the Israelites forward with unfaltering faith when all seemed lost. It was he who led them back to the mountain which, to him, must have seemed the very dwelling place of the LORD who had delivered them. It must surely have been at Mt Sinai, and at their common grazing ground at Kadesh that Moses taught the tribes of Israel to worship and obey the LORD who had 'brought them up out of the land of Egypt, from the house of bondage'. This was the period when the faith of Moses began, however falteringly, to become the faith of Israel also. And with the birth of that common faith a nation was born.

The Covenant at Sinai (Exod. xix., xx. 1–21)

Exod. xix. 3–6 gives a very clear account of the Covenant between God and Israel. Of course we need not believe that Moses heard God speaking those very words. This is an Old Testament writer's attempt to summarize the teaching which Moses gave to the Israelites when they reached Mt Sinai. The writer knew that Moses was the first great prophet of the LORD, the leader of his people in the days of their deliverance from Egypt. He knew, too, that the most deeply cherished religious beliefs of his people had come down to them from the days of Moses. He felt sure, therefore, that Moses must have spoken such words as these and that he must have spoken them in the name of the LORD. This was the religious faith

MOSES, THE PROPHETIC LEADER AND LAWGIVER 49

of Moses which, through his teaching, became the faith of Israel also.

This great statement of religious faith begins with the words: 'Ye have seen what I did . . . now therefore . . .'. The faith of Israel was based on a series of historical events. It was Israel's response to God's act of deliverance. Moses taught them to recognize God's action in the circumstances of their escape and he led them into a solemn covenant with the LORD who had delivered them. He taught them that they owed obedience and gratitude to God for what He had done. They were to be a people different from all other peoples. The nations of the world would be brought to a knowledge of God through them: 'Ye shall be a peculiar treasure . . . a kingdom of priests'. These beliefs about God's relationship with Israel, clearly expressed in this passage, are all quite central to the religious faith of the Old Testament. It was through such teaching as this that the faith of Moses must have begun to become the faith of Israel. As the tribes gathered at the sacred mountain, listened to the teaching of Moses, and joined in worship of the LORD, the faith of Israel took shape and the soul of a nation was born.

The manner in which Israel was to obey God is set out clearly in the Ten Commandments. They form the foundation stone of that great body of moral, social and religious laws which Jewish tradition links with the name of Moses. Not all of these laws can have come down from the days of Moses. Many of them are closely similar to laws which were common, at that time, in agricultural and commercial communities throughout western Asia. Even the Ten Commandments may have been developed in later centuries beyond the original teaching of Moses. We find, for instance, that Exod. xx. 8–11 and Deut. v. 12–15 give different reasons for the law of the Sabbath. Perhaps neither was present in the original statement. But there can be little doubt that the essential moral principles outlined in the Ten Commandments go back to Moses himself.

The stories of the desert period recognize very clearly that the faith of the people was fitful and faltering. No doubt it would reach a high pitch of enthusiasm at Mt Sinai. The memory of their wonderful escape would still be vivid. The awe-inspiring influences of the volcanic mountain, the power of Moses' own religious convictions and the solemn associations of the religious rite in which they sealed their covenant with the LORD (Exod. xxiv. 1–8) would stir profound emotions of reverence and devotion. But the books of Exodus and Numbers contain ample evidence that the enthusiasm quickly waned and their gratitude was soon forgotten. Hosea's eighth-century picture of his people's religious faith was true from the beginning: it was 'as a morning cloud and as the early dew it goeth away' (Hos. vi. 4).

Moses, the Man of God (Exod. xxxiii. 7–11; xxxiv. 29–35)

The faith of the people needed to be constantly renewed and sustained by the faith of their leader, and Moses, in turn, needed to find renewal of his own faith through frequent periods of prayer and meditation. There are two passages in the book of Exodus which preserve the memory of that fact very beautifully. The first (Exod. xxxiii. 7–11) tells of Moses' regular practice of prayer. In order to appreciate the full meaning of it we need to read it in the R.V., or in a modern translation. The Hebrew verb in v. 7 is in the imperfect tense and the passage is therefore describing a habitual practice. Whenever the nomadic Israelites pitched their tents at some new pasture ground in the desert Moses 'used to take ... and pitch' a special tent at some distance from the camp. This tent was recognized as a sacred place where Moses met with God. The people watched with awe as Moses walked towards the tent and, when he had entered, it seemed as if the very glory of God came down like a cloud (cf. pp. 11, 38) upon the tent and they knew that the LORD was speaking with Moses.

The second passage (Exod. xxxiv. 29–35) describes very beautifully the effect on Moses of those times when he withdrew to be alone with God. It refers first to a particular occasion. Israelite tradition had preserved the memory of a period when Moses ascended the mountain to commune with God and then returned and taught the people the laws by which the LORD wanted them to live. And it was remembered

MOSES, THE PROPHETIC LEADER AND LAWGIVER 51

that when he came down and began to teach them 'his face shone'. But the passage is not concerned with a single occasion only. It tells us that on that first occasion Moses put a veil over his face when he had finished speaking to the people but it goes on to say that 'he used to take' (the Hebrew verb is again in the imperfect tense) the veil off his face when he 'went in before the LORD to speak with him' and the Israelites saw his face shine whenever he came out again to teach them.

Such passages preserve, in a very beautiful and convincing way, the impression which Moses left upon the people of his own day. He was remembered as a man who lived in close and constant contact with God Himself. We need not take these passages in a literal and prosaic way. We all know how joy can cause anyone's face to 'light up' and sometimes we see a look of deeper joy and serenity in the eyes of those to whom prayer is a familiar practice. No doubt it was such a look which the Israelites saw on the face of Moses. And it would be no mere outer appearance. Those times when Moses went apart to be with God would leave their mark also on Moses' character. How else did the fiery and impetuous young man who slew the Egyptian overseer become the wise leader and lawgiver of Israel? Moses was not just a great military leader, a great statesman and a great moral and religious teacher. He must certainly have had outstanding qualities in all these directions. But above all Moses was remembered as a man in whom his people saw, reflected as in a mirror, the very glory of God Himself. And it is worth noticing that Joshua, who followed him as leader of the Israelites, apparently fulfilled some priestly office in the sacred tent where Moses met God. At this formative stage of their religious faith the Israelites needed leaders who had a deep personal trust in God and who lived in constant dependence on Him.

Chapter 6

JOSHUA, MILITARY LEADER AND MISSIONARY

God's promise to Joshua (Joshua i. 1–9)

Moses led the Israelites out of Egypt but Joshua was their leader when they entered Canaan. Moses had died in the desert but it was remembered of Joshua that he, too, was a man of great courage and confidence who committed himself in trust to God. He is said to have been one of the only two survivors among the men who had left Egypt under Moses (Num. xxvi. 65). All the others had died in the desert. He had proved himself as a leader in battle (Exod. xvii. 8–13) and he had been associated with Moses in leadership before the latter's death (Num. xxvii. 15–23). He was not of the same spiritual stature as Moses. God did not talk with him 'face to face' as he did with Moses (cf. Exod. xxxiii. 11 with Num. xxvii. 21) but he was well fitted for the task of leadership which awaited him. Later generations remembered him as a man who had clearly been called of God to the leadership of the Israelites at this new stage of their history. They found ample confirmation of that conviction in the events which followed.

The Jordan crossing (Joshua iii.)

When Moses died the Israelites were encamped on the plains of Moab, on the east side of the Jordan. The early attempt to enter Canaan from the south had long since been abandoned. Now they were prepared for a new attempt. Shittim was on the fringe of the Jordan valley and probably about seven miles from the river itself. A small mound still marks the spot and from that vantage point the Israelites must have gazed eagerly across the valley towards their new home.

The account of Joshua's leadership at this point of the story reminds us of Moses at the Red Sea crossing. The waters of the Jordan were in flood. That fact must have been known

JOSHUA, MILITARY LEADER AND MISSIONARY 53

to the Israelites for their flocks would be grazing along the river side. There were fords across the river but they would be too deep for safe passage while the floods lasted. It was a strange time to choose for an attempted crossing. Yet Joshua faced this formidable obstacle with sublime confidence: 'sanctify yourselves for tomorrow the LORD will do great things among you' (Judges iii. 5). The Ark of the LORD was

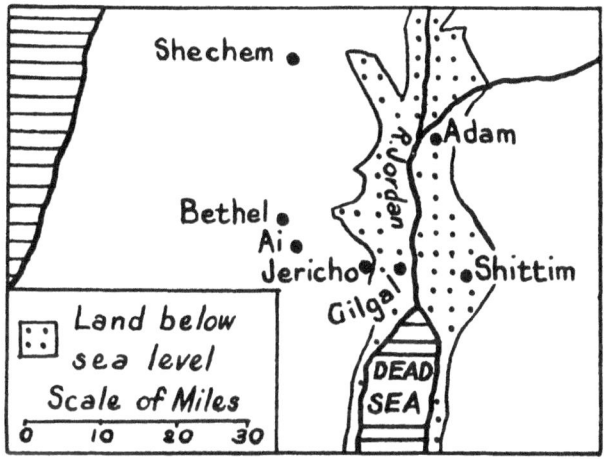

Joshua's entry into Canaan

to be carried in front by the priests and all the people were to follow them towards the river. This Ark, a simple wooden chest carried by two wooden poles attached to it, was a sacred object in the eyes of the Israelites. It symbolized for them the presence of the LORD among them. And so it must have seemed to them as if the LORD Himself were leading them towards the flood waters of the Jordan.

The events which followed have an obvious historical explanation. The R.V. text of Joshua iii. 16 reads: 'The waters which came down from above stood, and rose up in one heap, a great way off, at Adam, the city that is beside Zarethan'. This more accurate rendering provides an important clue.

Adam has been identified with Tell-el-Damieh, about sixteen miles up the river, near an important ford. Twice within the present century a serious landslide has occurred at this point. In 1927 an earthquake caused the west bank of the river to collapse and there was no water in the river bed south of Damieh for nearly twenty-four hours. It is just such a damming of the waters by a landslide that the text seems to describe. Did Joshua have information about the condition of the river bed at Adam which led him to anticipate this event? Did he see in it a providential opportunity for a surprise attack on the fortress town of Jericho which lay across the path of their advance into the hills of the promised land? It is impossible to answer such questions but it is equally impossible to miss the note of religious conviction which the passage contains, 'Hereby ye shall know that the living God is among you'. To Joshua and his followers, as to the generations that came after them, the crossing of the Jordan was signal evidence of the LORD's presence and power among them.

The standing stones at Gilgal (Joshua iv.)

About halfway between Jericho and the Jordan lies Jiljulieh, which is believed to be the site of Gilgal. The name Gilgal probably means 'the circle' and the definite article is always used with it in Hebrew (i.e. 'the Gilgal'). In the book of Amos it is criticized as a centre of idolatrous worship (Amos iv. 4). No trace of standing stones has yet been found on the site but it looks as if there had once been a stone circle of the Stonehenge type at this spot. It may have been a Canaanite sacred place before the Israelites arrived and the story of Joshua's twelve memorial stones may have grown up in an attempt to link the ancient shrine with the events of Israel's history. If the Israelites found the stones there when they crossed the river they may well have accepted them as an appropriate memorial by which all generations could be reminded of the Jordan crossing.

The capture of Jericho (Joshua vi.)

The site of Jericho has proved, and is still proving, a fascinating field of study for the archaeologist. Excavations have uncovered evidence of human habitation as far back as the neolithic period (4–3000 B.C.) and the remains of five successive cities have been discovered, dating from about 3000 B.C. to the ninth century B.C. The fourth of these cities seems to be the one of which we read in the book of Joshua. Much work has still to be done before the archaeologists can give us reliable information about the town of Joshua's day and the manner of its destruction. It is possible, however, to form a pretty clear picture of the appearance it must have presented to the Israelite invaders.

Jericho must have seemed a formidable obstacle to nomadic tribes from the desert. Its total circumference would only be about 650 yards but it was probably surrounded by double walls made of sun-dried brick. These walls probably rose to about 30 feet in height and they would be six to twelve feet thick. Houses built on the city walls (cf. Joshua ii:15) would give the place a still more imposing look. They would not be so strong as they seemed because they would stand on the debris of earlier ruins. Nevertheless Jericho would be an obstacle which desert warriors could have had little hope of overcoming. No ordinary power could have destroyed walls of such great thickness.

The archaeologists cannot yet say confidently when and how the walls collapsed. There is certainly ample evidence of destruction and fire on the site. An archaeologist's field report of March 1930 (quoted in *Garstang and Garstang: The Story of Jericho:* 1948 Edition: p.136) reads as follows: 'Investigations along the west side show continuous signs of destruction and conflagration. The outer wall suffered most, its remains falling down the slope. The inner wall is preserved only where it abuts upon the citadel, or tower, to a height of eighteen feet; elsewhere it is found largely to have fallen, together with the remains of buildings upon it, into the space between the walls which was filled with ruins and debris.' Later investigation has made it doubtful how that evidence should be dated and interpreted. It seems probable, however, that the story in Joshua vi is based on the memory of an actual event which

removed a serious obstacle from the path of Israelite invaders.
What caused the walls to fall? The archaeological evidence seems to suggest earthquake disturbance and it may be significant that the story of the Jordan crossing points in the same direction. It is quite possible that both events were due, historically, to a series of earthquake shocks following each other in close succession. The experience of such earth tremors and their remarkable results would certainly leave a profound impression on the Israelite tribes. It is certainly quite clear that the story in the book of Joshua had its origin in a dramatic historical occurrence in which the Israelites saw further evidence of God's presence and power.

The date of Jericho's destruction

An awkward problem of dating arises when we attempt to establish a close link between the archaeological evidence and the Biblical story. The archaeologists cannot give us a definite date for the final destruction of Jericho but it seems quite clear that it must have taken place between about 1475 B.C. and about 1300 B.C. If the Exodus took place at about 1450 B.C., as some Old Testament scholars suggest, the fall of Jericho would fit readily into the sequence of events. On the other hand there is definite archaeological evidence of the destruction of Bethel (Judges i. 22–5), Lachish (Joshua x. 31f.) and Debir (Joshua xv. 15–17; Judges i. 11–13) during the thirteenth century B.C. and there are other good reasons for believing that that was the period of Israelite invasion.

Difficulties such as these remind us again that the Biblical story cannot be regarded as a trustworthy record of the historical course of events. Archaeology has shown most convincingly that the record is based on actual historical happenings but there is evidence in the Bible itself that the Israelite conquest of Canaan was a much more gradual and more complex affair than a hasty reading of the book of Joshua might suggest. It is likely that there was more than one wave of Israelite invasion and events originally widely separated in time may have been linked together in later tradition to form a continuous story. As we have recognized before it was the religious meaning of the events which mattered most to the Bible writers.

The sacrificial destruction of the city (Joshua vi. 21-4)

The religious meaning of the fall of Jericho, to the Israelite tribes, is illustrated in the subsequent destruction of the city by fire. It is a terrible, and revolting, story of ruthless fanatical destruction. Yet to these primitive warriors the destruction of Jericho by fire was an act of solemn religious meaning. They were not taking a fierce revenge on their enemies. They were not enjoying destruction and bloodshed for their own sakes. They were acknowledging before the LORD, in their primitive way, that he had given them the first fruits of victory in the promised land. Just as the firstborn of their animals were offered to the LORD in sacrifice so this first city to be conquered in Canaan must be devoted to the LORD. They must not enrich themselves with the spoils of its conquest. The victory was the LORD's and the whole city must be offered to him in the fires of sacrifice. It is a truly terrible story but it does at least show how, in their fanatical and primitive way, the Israelites acknowledged that it was the LORD who had opened the way for them into the promised land of Canaan.

The conquest of Ai (Joshua viii. 1-29)

The story of the conquest of Ai presents another awkward problem of dating. The town has been identified with remains discovered about thirteen miles west of Jericho. But this town was completely destroyed before 2000 B.C. and the site was uninhabited until after 1200 B.C. It must, therefore, have been in ruins at the period of the Israelite invasion. It is possible that the writer has confused Ai with Bethel. There is no account of the capture of Bethel in Joshua but it is mentioned in Judges i. 22-5 and we know from archaeological evidence that the town of Bethel was destroyed at this time. It has also been suggested that the site of Ai was still a useful rallying point for defence. The name Ai means 'ruin' and the Canaanites may have gathered their forces behind the ruins in defence against the victorious Israelites. According to the

Bible story the stronghold was gained by stratagem and Joshua's skill as a military commander was clearly disclosed. The approach to the central plateau was opening up before the Israelites.

The archaeologists are still at work and much fresh light may still be thrown on the Biblical stories of the Israelite invasion of Canaan. New discoveries may compel the archaeologists to make further changes in the dates they now give for the destruction of the cities which figure in the books of Joshua and Judges. Other explanations may be offered for the collapse of the walls of Jericho. It is clear, however, from careful study of the Bible itself that we need not expect to be able to reconstruct a continuous and self-consistent account of the Israelite conquest and settlement in Canaan. As we have already seen it is likely that some Israelite tribes remained in Canaan from the days of Abraham and Jacob and it is possible that the later attack, which we associate with Joshua, was a prolonged affair which may have included several distinct waves of invasion.

The covenant at Shechem (Joshua xxiv.)

Although historical reconstruction may never be possible the last chapter of Joshua enables us to reconstruct the probable course of religious development. In this chapter we are given a picture of Joshua summoning representatives of all the tribes of Israel to meet with him at Shechem. The conquest is assumed to be complete and the land has been divided among the twelve tribes. Shechem was apparently already a recognized sanctuary, although the book of Joshua contains no account of a conquest of Shechem. At this established shrine Joshua called upon the twelve tribes to make a solemn choice of religious loyalty and he affirmed that he and his household would serve the LORD.

Joshua offered the tribes a threefold choice. They were asked to decide between the gods whom their fathers had worshipped in Mesopotamia, the local gods of the Canaanite peoples and the LORD who had delivered their fathers from Egypt. It may well be that Hebrew tribes who remained in

JOSHUA, MILITARY LEADER AND MISSIONARY

Canaan may have continued to follow the religious beliefs and practices of their ancestors in Mesopotamia. Shechem may even have been a centre of such worship. The Canaanite cults proved a powerful attraction to the Israelites for many centuries after Joshua and the Hebrew tribes who lived continuously in Canaan may have come under their influence before the days of Joshua. But a powerful new religious influence entered Canaan with the Israelite tribes who had escaped from Egypt.

Joshua and his followers were ardent missionaries of a new faith. They were aflame with zeal for the LORD who had delivered them and had brought them to the land of promise. Although the Israelites of later history were a people of mixed physical ancestry they acknowledged a common spiritual inheritance. They all worshipped the LORD who had delivered their ancestors from Egypt. It looks as if this last chapter in the book of Joshua preserves the memory of an actual historical achievement. The powerful missionary impulses of Joshua and his followers may have kindled a response from the kindred tribes among whom they settled when they entered Canaan. That challenge to decision had to be sounded again centuries later (cf. 1 Kings xviii. 21). Joshua and his contemporaries had long since passed away and new generations had arisen 'which knew not the LORD nor yet the works which he had done for Israel' (Judges ii. 10). The fascination of Canaanite baal worship proved too strong for the Israelites and for centuries a struggle went on between the old desert traditions and the nature cults of Canaan. But the new faith had been securely planted in the land and the story of the covenant at Shechem provides an appropriate ending to the Biblical account of the entry into Canaan.

Part III

GOD AND MAN
IN THE FOUNDING OF A KINGDOM

CHAPTER 7

SAMUEL, RELIGIOUS LEADER IN TIME OF CRISIS

Consequences of the settlement in Canaan (Judges i. 19-21, 27-36; ii. 7-19)

The book of Judges preserves for us a number of old traditions about tribal leaders in the period of the settlement in Canaan. They give us a picture of a troubled period when Canaan was subject to successive attacks from eastern invaders. The land was still nominally under the sovereignty of Egypt but Egyptian power was waning and no other imperial power had taken her place. In this situation the Israelites seem gradually to have attained a position of leadership by defending the land against alien peoples. Only two of the six chief 'judges' of whom we read, were leaders in a struggle against Canaanite peoples. The rest were engaged in struggles against invaders. It is clear, however, that the authority of these 'judges' was local and temporary. The editor of the book of Judges gives us a fair summary of the period when he suggests that the old desert faith was the one force which held the Israelite tribes together during this period. When no danger threatened this unity was lost but in face of a common foe the faith of their fathers stirred them to united and effective action (cf. Judges ii. 11-19).

The Israelite tribes which had escaped from slavery in Egypt under Moses and entered Canaan under Joshua had now settled down in their new home. The great event of the Exodus and the entry into Canaan belonged to the past. The conquest had not been complete. The Canaanites had walled cities and iron chariots against which the lightly equipped desert warriors had fought in vain. Judges i. 19-21, 27-36 shows that the Israelite tribes had to settle down among the peoples already in Canaan. They were separated from one another by geographical barriers and by hostile peoples. Each tribe had its own problems to face and its own difficulties to overcome. Many Israelite families had given up the old shepherd life and had become farmers. In copying the farming practices of the Canaanites they had begun to adopt the debasing fertility cults by which the Canaanites sought to secure good harvests. They were forgetting the LORD who had brought them out of the land of Egypt, and they were worshipping the local gods and goddesses of the land, the baalim and the ashtaroth (Judges xxii. 11-13).

The coming of the Philistines
Towards the end of the period covered by the book of Judges a new and more serious danger threatened from the west. The stories of Samson tell of exploits against the Philistines. They were a warlike people who had established themselves on the southern coast of Canaan during the twelfth century B.C. They were survivors of the old Aegean civilization and they possessed the resources of an advanced culture. During the eleventh century they began to spread their influence over the whole country. With the decay of Egyptian power there did not seem to be any reason why they should not gain control of the whole land and, for a time, it looked as if Canaan might become the land of the Philistines. A crisis had arisen which threatened the very survival of the Israelite faith. If the Philistines had established an empire in Canaan the Israelite tribes might not have survived as an independent people. Like the ancient Britons in England they might have been scattered by the powerful invaders and their religious traditions might have been forgotten.

The religious leadership of Samuel
In this critical situation 'the word of the LORD came' to Samuel (1 Sam. iii. 21). This phrase is a characteristic one in Old Testament history. At successive crises in Israel's story we see men appearing who give the creative leadership which the situation demands. Each one of them speaks and acts in the name of the LORD. Each one is possessed by the conviction that God has called him. Each one commits

himself in complete trust to the will and purpose of God. They are the figures whom we call the prophetic leaders of Israel. Moses was the first, the human founder of Israel's faith. Samuel may be regarded as the second outstanding figure of this type. Elijah is the next and then we come to the men whose teaching has been preserved for us in the Old Testament books which we call the books of the prophets. Every one of them was a man of 'faith'. They were all creative leaders in times of crisis because they were sensitive to the great spiritual issues of their age. They did not seek personal power or profit. They responded without reserve to the call of God. It was through such men that the nature and purpose of God was disclosed and the way was prepared for the coming of Jesus in whom the word of the LORD was 'made flesh' (John i. 14).

The historical Samuel

The stories of Samuel in the Old Testament present us with a familiar difficulty. Samuel was certainly a real historical individual but it is difficult to penetrate behind the Biblical record of his activities and reconstruct the likely course of historical events. It is difficult to distinguish between historical reality and religious tradition. There are a number of references in the books of Samuel and Kings to companies of prophets (sometimes called 'the sons of the prophets') and it seems clear that bands of fanatical religious enthusiasts were a familiar feature of Israelite society at this time. Some of them probably possessed those unusual powers, such as 'second sight' which are being studied by psychologists nowadays. All of them were in the habit of stimulating one another to frenzies of religious excitement during which they spoke and acted as if possessed by supernatural powers. Such prophetic bands were not confined to Israelite society, nor were they to be found only among the worshippers of the LORD. We read of prophets of the baalim in the Bible and this type of ecstatic behaviour (see 1 Kings xviii. 26, 28), seems to have been a feature of Canaanite religion. It is clear, however, that the bands of prophets of the LORD played an important part in the revival of the desert traditions among the Israelites when the Philistine danger was reaching its height. We cannot be sure whether Samuel belonged to this class of ecstatic prophet or whether he used their efforts for the furtherance of national and religious unity. It is clear, at least, that Samuel was remembered by later generations as the religious leader through whose initiative the Philistine danger was eventually overcome and an Israelite kingdom securely established in the 'promised land'.

There are two quite distinct and, in some respects, self-contradictory pictures of Samuel given to us in the Bible. In 1 Samuel vii. we see him as the acknowledged leader and lawgiver of 'all the house of Israel'. Under his leadership the Israelites return to the faith of their fathers and God grants them a great and decisive victory over the Philistines. In the ninth chapter, however, Saul apparently knows nothing about Samuel. In this chapter he appears as a 'seer' of whom Saul learns from his servant. Instead of being a national figure he is a man with a local reputation for second sight.

These contradictory pictures are due to the composite character of the books of Samuel. They reached their present form as a result of editorial work by more than one hand. They certainly contain a good deal of valuable historical material which must have been written at an early date but there is also later material which is coloured by the outlook of a later age. It is difficult to be sure, therefore, what precise historical part Samuel played in the events of this critical period or whether he was widely known in his own generation. We may be sure, however, that his spiritual leadership was decisive. He led the revival of Israel's religious traditions. He united the tribes in defence of these traditions and he gave them their first king. On these grounds alone later tradition was justified in seeing Samuel as a great prophetic leader. In a time of crisis the word of the LORD did come to Samuel and he responded in trust and obedience.

The story of Samuel's childhood and adolescence (1 Sam. i; ii, 1–11; iii.)

Samuel is introduced to us in the Bible as the child of devout parents who is dedicated to service in the temple of the LORD from his birth. Elkahnah and Hannah lived near the sanctuary

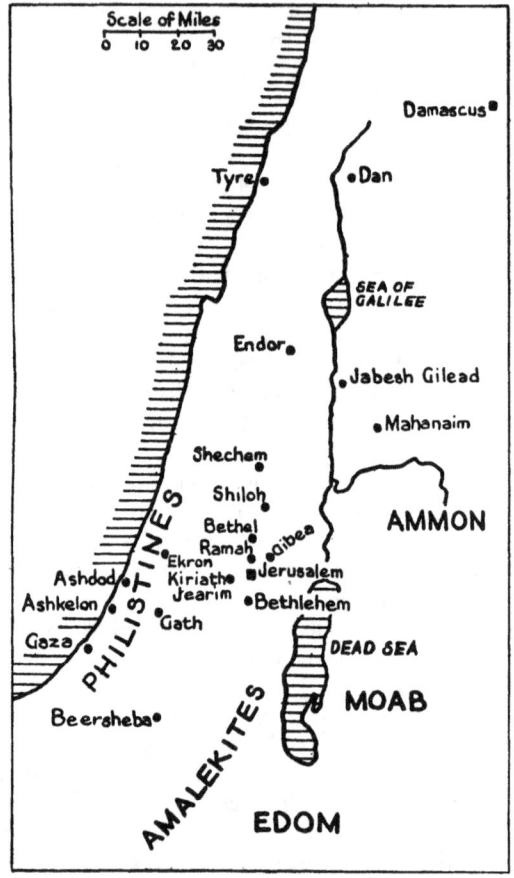

Israel in the time of Samuel and Saul

of Shiloh in the hill country of Ephraim. Hannah was childless and she prayed earnestly that God would give her a son, vowing that the son would be dedicated to the LORD. The child was

SAMUEL, RELIGIOUS LEADER IN TIME OF CRISIS 67

born and in due course was brought to the sanctuary at Shiloh and given into the care of Eli the priest.

The 'temple' at Shiloh was apparently a well-established and important centre of Israelite worship at this time. The sacred Ark of the LORD was housed in it and the annual religious festivals were celebrated there. There seems to have been a small staff of priests and attendants and a regular routine of sacrificial worship. Samuel was given into Eli's charge in order that he might be trained for priestly service at the sanctuary.

The familiar story in chapter three shows how Samuel's dedication to the LORD in infancy was confirmed by a personal religious experience in adolescence. No age is mentioned but the story makes it clear that Samuel was already old enough to take some small part in the temple services when his mother first left him with Eli and we are told that three sons and two daughters were born to Hannah during the period before this incident occurred. The story describes very simply and beautifully the awakening of a personal knowledge of God. There is a stage in early childhood when the word 'ought' begins to have an authority which is not derived merely from the parents. When his father or mother says 'you ought to do this' or 'you ought not to do that' the child begins to realize that it is not merely the command of his parent which he is being called upon to obey. He begins to feel within himself an answering 'Yes, I know that I ought', or 'I know that I ought not'. That same experience of moral challenge or rebuke which does not come merely from parents or from social conventions is felt more clearly in adolescence and it plays a central part in religious awakening. This story may be taken as symbolizing such a religious awakening. The voice, which Samuel had assumed to be the voice of Eli, is recognized as the voice of God. Children learn about God from their parents and teachers but some personal experience is necessary before religious faith can play a decisive part in the lives of men and women.

Samuel was remembered as a man who, from his childhood, had clearly been marked out as a spiritual leader and teacher.

He had learned early to listen for the voice of God and he had shown in his youth that self-forgetful courage which enables the great spiritual leaders of men to speak and to act fearlessly in obedience to the truth that has been revealed to them. He did not shrink from exposing to Eli the unpalatable consequences of his two sons' wicked behaviour. These pictures of Samuel, in his infancy and in his adolescence, preserve for us the impression which Samuel left on the memory of his people. 'And all Israel . . . knew that Samuel was established to be a prophet of the LORD'.

Samuel as a national leader (1 Sam. vii. 5–17; viii.)

The story of the Philistine defeat at Mizpah and its consequences (vii. 5–17) cannot be reconciled with the known facts of history. In ix. 16 Samuel is guided by God to anoint Saul as king in order to deliver the Israelites from the Philistine menace and in xiv. 52 we are told that, 'there was sore war against the Philistines all the days of Saul'. The story in chapter four of the Israelite defeat with the capture of the Ark, the death of Eli and the tragic cry 'The glory is departed from Israel; for the ark of God is taken' gives a much truer picture of the probable course of events. The peaceful life at Shiloh was shattered by disastrous military defeat and the hour of crisis had struck for Israel.

Chapters seven and eight give us the later, idealized picture of Samuel as the national leader who ruled Israel as the representative of the LORD. By the time these chapters were being written Israel had suffered under many evil kings. As the historians of that later date looked back over the records of their people's history it seemed clear to them that the institution of the monarchy had been a mistake. The LORD was the true ruler of His people and evil consequences had come upon them ever since they had been ruled by human kings. They idealized the old days before the beginning of the monarchy. They pictured Samuel as the prophet, priest and judge who ruled over all the tribes of Israel in the name of the LORD. They described how he led the people in a great act of national repentance, in response to which the LORD gave them a

SAMUEL, RELIGIOUS LEADER IN TIME OF CRISIS 69

miraculous and decisive victory over their enemies: 'So the Philistines were subdued and they came no more into the coast of Israel: and the hand of the LORD was against the Philistines all the days of Samuel'. The foundation of the monarchy is then represented as the consequence of Israel's rebellious demands. Samuel is pictured granting the demands of the people most reluctantly and warning them of the consequences of their disloyalty to the LORD who is the true king of Israel.

Selection of Saul by the sacred lot (1 Sam. x. 17–27)

Chapter x. 17–27 continues this account of the origin of the monarchy and tells how Saul was selected. The method used, according to this tradition, was the method of the sacred lot. The Hebrew word translated 'was taken' is a technical term which conveys that meaning. The same procedure was followed in the incident recorded in xiv. 38–42. The Greek text has a variant reading of this passage which helps to throw light on this ancient Hebrew method of seeking divine guidance. Two objects seem to have been used, called the Urim and the Thummim (see Exod. xxviii. 30 and Ezra ii. 63). These may have been small stones of distinctive colour or shape and it is possible that the ephod (cf. 1 Sam. xxi. 9; xxiii. 6) may have been a receptacle for these objects, habitually worn by the priests as part of their sacred dress. When questions were put, the ephod may have been shaken and an aperture may have allowed one or other of the objects to fall out (cf. Joshua xvi. 1; xix. 1). The question would need to be framed in such a way as to permit of a clear choice between two possibilities. Each stone would stand for one of these two possibilities and the colour, or shape, of the stone which fell out would reveal the decision between them.

The historical origin of the monarchy (1 Sam ix. 1 to x. 16; xi. 1–11, 15)

The probable course of history is indicated much more clearly in the second account of the origin of the monarchy. It is contained in xi. 1 to x. 16; xi. 1–11, 15 and is undoubtedly the older of the two accounts. The editor of the book of Samuel wove the two accounts together and added some verses and phrases of his own to try to make a coherent whole. This earlier version tells how Saul was secretly anointed by Samuel and subsequently acclaimed by the people after he had proved his military prowess by a daring act of leadership. The story of Saul seeking his father's asses and meeting with Samuel suggests that Samuel was a passive agent of God's purposes who was suddenly called upon to act in response to a 'supernatural' revelation. There are indications in the chapter, however, which help us to realize how Samuel may have been led to act as he did.

The menace of the Philistines must have been obvious to any intelligent and responsible Israelite living in these times. All that we know of Samuel suggests that he, above all men, would be conscious of the critical situation. For him it would be a religious as well as a national concern. Such a man would surely seek the guidance of God in this critical situation. But he would not pray about it and then wait passively for God to give him some obvious guidance. He would realize the need for leadership and he would seek actively for evidence of it. Saul, we are told, was the son of 'a mighty man of valour'. The Hebrew really means that his father was a 'man of substance', a large landowner. Saul himself was apparently well fitted also by age and physical endowment to play a leader's part. It may well be that Samuel had heard of Saul as a likely leader before he set eyes on him. He may even have learned that Saul already cherished ambitions of leadership in this hour of danger. Is that, perhaps, the significance of the phrase 'all that is in thine heart' (ix. 19)? If that were so the news that Saul was in the neighbourhood and was actually coming to see him—however that news came to Samuel—would be recognized by him as the very act of God.

Such reconstruction is, of course, largely guesswork. But it is important to realize that Samuel and Saul were real figures of history whose experience of God came in just such ways as it comes to men and women today. Men still have striking and convincing experience of divine guidance. At times such experience may even be accompanied by visions or voices, as in the case of Joan of Arc, but it is not in such unusual accompaniments that we see evidence that God is really speaking to them. Samuel became the instrument of God in the selection of Saul to be king because in this time of crisis and danger he was spiritually alert and sensitive. The account of the 'signs' contained in x. 2–7 reinforces the feeling of magic and mystery which the passage conveys but there is no reason to assume that there was anything magical about the guidance which Samuel received. Samuel was sensitive to the spiritual consequences of the Philistine menace. He sought the guidance of God and he used, we may be sure, his own resources of wisdom and enquiry. He was convinced that God Himself had guided him to the selection of Saul as the ideal leader who could unite the Israelite tribes in their hour of danger. And so he anointed him in the name of the LORD.

The conflict between Samuel and Saul (1 Sam. xiii. 7*b*–15*a*; xv.)

Although Samuel had selected Saul as king a sharp conflict soon developed between the two men. Two accounts of that conflict are given in the Bible. The first tells how Saul, in a desperate emergency, offered sacrifice before battle in the absence of Samuel. By doing so he trespassed on Samuel's priestly responsibilities and he incurred a sharp rebuke for his action. The second account is given at greater length, and describes a more blatant act of disobedience. In both accounts Samuel tells Saul that God has rejected him because of his disobedience. The LORD has chosen another king and the throne of Israel will pass from the house of Saul after his death.

A 'holy war' against the Amalekites (1 Sam. xv.)

The fuller account of Saul's rejection tells of a command given by Samuel in the name of the LORD. The Amalekites were a nomadic people who lived to the south of Palestine. They were old enemies of the Israelites (see Exod. xvii. 8; Num. xiv. 45; Judges vi. 3) and now Saul was commanded to lead an expedition against them and destroy them. It was to be a 'holy war'. These Amalekites were not to be regarded just as tribal enemies. They were to be regarded as enemies of the LORD and the LORD Himself would give the victory to His people. There must be, therefore, no personal profit from the battle. No spoil was to be taken. The Amalekites were all to be slain and their possessions were to be utterly destroyed.

Saul's disobedience.
The story tells that Saul carried out a successful attack but that he did not obey Samuel's command. He spared Agag, the king of the Amalekites, and he kept the best of the flocks and herds. The motives of his action become clear enough as the story proceeds. 'I feared the people and obeyed their voice', he said. Saul was certainly not prompted by feelings of mercy. He wanted to be popular with his troops and he was unwilling to deny them the spoils of victory. No doubt he had also pictured the effect on his people if he were seen returning triumphantly from the battle with Agag as his captive. Saul valued the personal power and prestige of the kingly office and he was forgetting that that office was God's gift and that God's commands must govern all his actions.

The rejection of Saul
Samuel belonged to a primitive age and his command to Saul sounds to us like the voice of human hatred and vengeance. In the light of New Testament teaching it is impossible for us to believe that God really commanded the slaughter of the Amalekites. But Saul recognized Samuel to be a prophet of God. For Saul a command from Samuel was a command of the LORD. And Saul had consciously and deliberately disobeyed. He had set aside the divine command, as he understood it, in order to gratify his own feelings of kingly power. Samuel had much to learn about the nature of God. The revelation of God's love in Jesus Christ, with all that that means for human relationships, still lay in the future. But Samuel had clear convictions about the duties and responsibilities of an Israelite king. No man was fit to be king who let his own selfish interests sway his

actions. Saul had failed and a new king must be found. The rejection of Saul raises some interesting and perplexing questions. Did God really choose Saul to be king? Did Samuel make a mistake or did God not know that Saul would prove a failure? The initial choice and subsequent rejection of Saul certainly seems to have been a problem which exercised the minds of the Old Testament historians. It seemed clear to them that Saul must have sinned most grievously since he was not succeeded on the throne by one of his own family and they say, quite simply, that 'the LORD repented that he had made Saul king over Israel', that is that God wished He had not done so!

Prophets and Kings in Old Testament history

The conflict between Samuel and Saul is the first instance of a characteristic feature in Old Testament history. The voice of the prophet is frequently heard criticizing the conduct of Old Testament kings, and sometimes verbal criticism passes over into political action. The prophets of Israel were like the conscience of the nation and kings, as well as commoners, came under judgement. Deut. xvii. 14–20 gives a striking picture of the qualities and behaviour which should be expected of an Israelite king and the Old Testament writers judge all kings by that standard. The kings of Israel were the anointed of the LORD and they ruled over a people who were in covenant with the LORD. They must therefore be obedient in all things to the commandments of the LORD. They must rule in accordance with God's laws. The faith of Israel shaped the Old Testament conception of Israel's king and of the Israelite kingdom. No such perfect king ever appeared in Israelite history but Israel's prophets taught their people to hope for a messianic king who would give perfect obedience to God and through whom God's perfect rule ('the kingdom of God') would be established among the nations.

CHAPTER 8

DAVID THE WARRIOR

The ideal king of Israel's golden age

The Old Testament historians looked back to Moses as the founder and lawgiver of their nation and they saw in David the architect of their political and religious life. He was the true founder of the political kingdom. Where Saul had failed David had succeeded. Under his able leadership the Philistine menace was broken and the kingdom of Israel was firmly established in the land of promise. He captured Jerusalem and made it the centre of national and religious life. He planned the building of the Temple, although the actual work was carried out in the reign of Solomon his son. His religious interests and his poetic achievement associated his name inseparably with the Psalms, which eventually played so large a part in Temple worship. Later generations looked back on him as the ideal king of Israel's golden age.

There is a great wealth of information about David in the Bible and most of it is based on contemporary records. 2 Sam. ix.–xx. reads like a consecutive story and it is generally regarded as a continuous document which has come down to us from David's own day. The writer seems to have had first-hand information about the events which he describes so vividly and it is quite possible that he may have shared in these events himself. The record of David's earlier life is much more complex and the hand of a later editor can be traced more frequently. Many stories would be told about a famous man like David and the eastern story-teller loves a colourful tale. One or two such stories probably found their way into the record along with more accurate material from official and contemporary writers. Sometimes a late editor may have touched up the portrait of David from motives of hero worship. But most of our knowledge of David is quite reliable and we can be quite confident about the type of man he was and about the part he played in the history of his people. We cannot fail to recognize the profound impression which David left on the memory of his people.

Samuel anoints David (1 Sam. xvi. 1–13)

David is introduced to us in three distinct ways. Chapter xvi. 1–13 tells us how Samuel was led to select and anoint him as king, in place of Saul. The second half of the same chapter tells us of his introduction at Saul's court and it contains no hint that David was conscious that he was destined to succeed the man into whose presence he had been brought and whose armour-bearer he became. In xvii. 12 David is again introduced by name, as if he were entirely unknown to the reader and in this story Saul is represented as inquiring who he is (cf. xvi. 21 with xvii. 55–8). There are discrepancies here which it is impossible to reconcile and it is quite obvious that the editor has combined material from several sources.

The editor's motive in beginning with the story of the anointing by Samuel is not difficult to understand. David is being introduced to us as 'the man after his own heart' (1 Sam. xiii. 14) whom the LORD had chosen in place of Saul. The incident shows Samuel in a new light. He is represented as hesitant and afraid and his own judgement is superficial and erroneous. The writer seems to be at pains to point out to us that the choice of David was not merely a human selection. Samuel acted as the agent of a divine insight which contradicted and overruled his personal judgement: 'Man looketh on the outward appearance but the LORD looketh on the heart', is clearly the key sentence in the passage.

The story of David and Goliath (1 Sam. xvii.)

1 Sam. xvii. introduces us to an interesting textual problem. The Greek version of the Old Testament contains a much shorter account of David and Goliath than the Hebrew version on which our English translation is based. It omits xvii. 12–31, 41, 50, 55–8; xviii. 1–5. Why should that be so? Were these verses in the Hebrew text when it was first written? While we cannot give a definite answer to that question we can

venture to express a pretty confident opinion. The earliest complete manuscript of the Hebrew Bible which we possess today dates only from the ninth century A.D., although we have substantial parts which take us a good deal farther back. We have much earlier manuscripts of the Greek version and we know that it was first translated from the Hebrew in the third and second centuries B.C. The Greek manuscript therefore shows us what the Hebrew text must have been when the translation was made. It seems probable, therefore, that the shorter version of this part of 1 Samuel is a more accurate picture of the original text. Many Old Testament scholars think that the additional verses in our English version were added to the Hebrew text from some independent and fuller account of the Goliath incident. When these verses are omitted the discrepancy between xvii. 55–8 and xvi. 21 disappears. David would naturally be in the Israelite camp as the king's armour-bearer and he shows his youthful courage by immediately volunteering to accept the Philistine's challenge.

The story of David and Goliath is rather like the story of Alfred and the cakes. It obviously belongs to popular tradition and we cannot be certain that it is historically reliable. In 2 Sam. xxi. 19 the original Hebrew text reads: 'and Elthanan ... slew Goliath the Gittite, the staff of whose spear was like a weaver's beam' (cf. 1 Sam. xvii. 7). Were there two such giants of the same name? Was the exploit of one of David's followers later attributed to the popular Israelite hero who had certainly delivered his people from the Philistine menace? Did David himself actually figure in some such heroic episode against a Philistine champion and did the two stories become confused in popular tradition? Such questions are interesting but they are comparatively unimportant. The story, as it has come down to us, reflects accurately one aspect of the picture of David which was cherished by subsequent generations and it helps us to recognize the impression which he made on the people of his own day.

The key verses in the passage are those which record the conversation between Saul and David and between David and the Philistine warrior. David had had no experience of battle but he had often faced danger in other forms. A shepherd's life in Palestine was subject to serious hazards from wild animals and from robbers. David had already proved his courage in that testing school. His words to the king would have a hint of youthful arrogance were it not for the fact that he claims no personal credit for his achievements. He recognized that it was 'the LORD that delivered' him from the lion and the bear. This simple religious faith comes out even more clearly in the conversation with Goliath. David met the giant's taunts with the confident claim that he came in the name of the LORD and the God of Israel would give him the victory.

The contrast between Saul and David (1 Sam. xviii. 1–16)

Here is an important aspect of David's character which has no real counterpart in the story of Saul. Saul seemed to have a good deal in common with the prophet bands of his period (1 Sam. x. 10–13). There is plenty of evidence of fanatical and turbulent religious emotion in his nature but he lacked the calm, trustful confidence which can be traced in David from the beginning. David, too, was a man of strong passions but there was also a deep serenity in him which had its source in religious faith.

The contrast between Saul and David comes out very clearly in their relationship with one another. David's youthful prowess won him many admirers and he quickly became a popular hero. Saul's jealousy was at once aroused. The story of Saul's victory over the Amalekites and disobedience to Samuel's instructions has already shown us how dependent he was on the good opinion of his followers. He disobeyed Samuel because he wanted to be popular with his soldiers. He lacked the inner confidence which comes from self-forgetful trust. He needed constant reassurance from the good opinion of others. Popular opinion now seemed to be turning away from him and towards David. His inner feelings of security were at once threatened, his prestige seemed to be at stake and he was ready even to believe that his throne was in danger. Jealousy bred envy and hatred and Saul tried to kill his young rival. David, on the other hand, betrayed neither fear nor resentment.

David and Jonathan (1 Sam. xx.)

The friendship between David and Jonathan is one of the most attractive features in the story of David. It seems to have sprung up from their earliest contacts with one another. There was such complete trust between them that David turned spontaneously to Jonathan to seek an explanation of Saul's enmity. Jonathan found it hard to believe that his father had any evil intentions towards David and he readily agreed to put Saul's feelings to a simple test. Verses 11–17 are generally regarded as a later insertion into the original story told in chapter xx. They certainly break the sequence of the narrative and it does not seem natural, at this point, that Jonathan should apparently foresee a coming reversal of fortune which would leave him at David's mercy.

Jonathan carried out the test and was shocked by the violence of Saul's anger. His father's angry passions broke out in a cruel and insulting taunt against Jonathan's own mother. He resented Jonathan's friendship with David so deeply that he was ready to insinuate that Jonathan was not really his own son. Stung to the quick by Saul's bitter words, Jonathan left the family table and sought out David. There could be no doubt about his father's feelings. David was clearly in serious danger. Jonathan gave the appointed signal which warned David that he must flee and the two friends bade each other a sorrowful farewell.

David as an outlaw (1 Sam. xxii. 1–2; xxiii. 14–18)

Saul had no palace but his family home was at Gibeah which lay ten or twelve miles in a north-westerly direction from Jerusalem. This seems to have been his normal residence throughout his reign and it was the centre of his simple court. David belonged to the tribe of Judah and his home was in Bethlehem. When he fled from the court he naturally sought refuge in familiar and friendly territory. Adullam lay among the hills some twelve miles to the south-west of Bethlehem. David was joined there by his relatives and by men who, like himself, were outlaws from their own nations. David became their natural leader and, in this way, he had early experience in the art of handling men. It would be no easy apprenticeship for his followers must have included many lawless and independent men.

Many exploits are told about David and his followers during this period. It was a time of constant danger and David was soon aware that Saul himself was seeking him out to kill him. Jonathan's loyalty to him, however, remained unswerving. There is a story which tells how Jonathan came to David with a message of encouragement and support. It seems likely that this story is unhistorical as, once again, it depicts Jonathan speaking of David as the future king. The picture it gives of Jonathan, however, is in keeping with all we know of him and it illustrates the unselfish friendship that existed between the two men. Jonathan's warmhearted and generous admiration for David stand out very clearly in his words. He had no thought for his own interests as Saul's son and natural heir. He rejoiced in David's prospects and he asked nothing better than to come second to David in the kingdom.

David spares Saul's life
Two stories are told of David's magnanimous action in sparing Saul's life. The two stories are closely similar although the details are different, and it seems likely that they are varying accounts of the same historical incident. The second is generally thought to be the older and more accurate version. It is fuller and it gives a finer picture of both Saul and David. Both accounts bring out the main features of the incident.

The first account (1 Sam. xxiv.)
In the first version Saul is shown in pursuit of David in a rocky area on the western shore of the Dead Sea. David and his men had taken refuge in the interior of an extensive cave, and Saul had come alone into the cave to meet the needs of nature. David's men urged him to seize the opportunity and

slay his enemy, but David was horrified at such a suggestion. Saul was the LORD's anointed. He had been solemnly set apart to the sacred office of the kingship and to David's religious nature an attack on the king's person would have seemed like an act of sacrilege. He did permit himself to cut off a portion of the king's garment, without disclosing his presence, in order that he might have proof that the king had been in his power but even that action gave him an uneasy conscience. When Saul had gone David followed him and revealed what he had done in the hope of proving to Saul that he had no evil ambitions. Saul's emotional nature was deeply moved by this proof of David's generous loyalty and he acknowledged that David had proved himself the finer man of the two. Saul's words here, however, are not historically convincing. It is not likely that he would have spoken so clearly and confidently of David's succession to the throne. His attempts to kill David seem pointless if he had this certain knowledge of the future course of events.

The second account (1 Sam. xxvi.)

The second account of David's forbearance is set in a barren area further north. The situation is so closely parallel that it would have been strange indeed if neither Saul nor David had alluded to the former incident. The only reasonable explanation of their silence is that the two stories have a common origin. The second account certainly gives a more dignified and heroic colour to the incident. The encounter, according to this version, was not accidental. It was the fruit of careful planning and bold action by David and his friends.

David and Abishai made their way to Saul's camp by night and found the whole camp asleep. A spear stuck in the ground marked the entrance to Saul's own tent and it would have been easy to kill Saul and escape without rousing his followers. In this instance, also, David repudiated such a proposal. At his suggestion they removed Saul's spear and a cruse of water and withdrew to a place of safety on the opposite hillside. From there David hailed Saul's general and taunted him for not keeping a safe watch over the king. Saul himself awoke

DAVID THE WARRIOR   81

and recognized David's voice in the darkness. A similar conversation followed between Saul and David as is reported in the former incident. On this occasion also Saul admitted his fault and acknowledged that David's action was evidence of his innocence and of great future achievement. There is no hint, however, regarding David's succession to the throne and the conversation has a much more convincing ring of originality.

Two accounts of Saul's death (1 Sam. xxxi.; 2 Sam. i. 1–10)

Saul died on the battlefield after a disastrous defeat by the Philistines. Two conflicting accounts of his death are given. In the last chapter of 1 Samuel we are told that his sons were slain and that he himself was wounded and in imminent danger of capture. He bade his armour-bearer kill him, lest he be taken by the Philistines and, when the armour-bearer refused to do so, Saul fell upon his sword and killed himself. The account in the opening chapter of 2 Samuel tells that an Amalekite, who reported Saul's death to David, claimed that he himself had slain Saul at his own request. It is thought likely that the former is the more trustworthy tradition. It seems significant that David's later references to this messenger makes no mention of him having slain Saul (see 2 Sam. iv. 9–11) although the context would have made it natural for him to include such a reference. Whatever the precise circumstances may have been the manner of Saul's death was tragic enough. The Philistine victory left the country at their mercy and Saul's unhappy reign ended in disastrous defeat.

David and the Philistine army (1 Sam. xxvii.; xxviii. 1–2; xxix.)

At the time of this battle David was actually serving as an officer in the Philistine army. He had taken refuge among the Philistines to secure their protection against Saul. In spite of Saul's fair words, spoken when David spared his life, David seems still to have felt that his life was in danger, and there was apparently no other step open to him. He could not live indefinitely as a fugitive and there was no other source of protection within the country. The Philistines gave Ziglag to David and his men and from that centre they raided the surrounding countryside as allies of the Philistine king. When the latter was gathering his army for the decisive battle against the Israelites he assumed that David and his followers would fight with him but his own officers objected. They were afraid that they might not be able to count on David's undivided loyalty. Thus David was saved from an awkward predicament and he himself was engaged in a raid against the Amalekites when the struggle was going on.

David's lament over Saul and Jonathan (2 Sam. xvii. 17–27)

The manner in which David received the news of the Philistine victory shows very clearly that his heart was with his own people and his lament over Saul and Jonathan shows conclusively that he had no personal ambition to succeed to the throne. Few scholars have questioned David's authorship and no one could doubt the sincerity of this moving elegy over his friend Jonathan and over his erstwhile enemy, who was nevertheless his king. The poem is one of the finest elegies in all literature. It is also one of the earliest. It was apparently preserved in a collection of poetry called the Book of Jasher (see also Joshua x. 13), and it was presumably quoted from that source by the Hebrew historian. The existing Hebrew text is not very good but the English translation has been finely done although the meaning is not always quite clear.

David becomes king over Judah (2 Sam., ii. 1–4)

The political situation after Saul's death is not very clear. The Philistines certainly had the whole land at their mercy and we read in 2 Sam. xxiii. 14 of the Philistine garrison actually occupying Bethlehem. It is possible that David really went to Hebron as a representative of the Philistines or, at least, with their good-will. Gath was the nearest of the five Philistine towns and it was with Achish, the king of Gath, that David and his men had been serving. The tribe of Judah would rally willingly round the popular figure of their own tribesman and the Philistines may have been well content to see Israelite allegiance divided. Saul's son, Ishbosheth, had his headquarters on the east side of the Jordan and he would command the allegiance of Benjamin and the tribes of the north. He, too, may have held a position of vassalage under the Philistines.

CHAPTER 9

DAVID THE KING

David becomes king over all Israel (2 Sam. iii. 1; v. 1-12)

The Bible tells us that David 'reigned over Judah seven years and six months', and there is no reason to doubt the accuracy of the statement. During the first two years there seem to have been frequent armed clashes between the forces of David and those of Ishbosheth. There was no comparison between the two leaders. Ishbosheth was completely overshadowed by David and was unable to command even the loyalty of his chief officer. Treachery and intrigue led eventually to the assassination of Ishbosheth two years after Saul's death. Jonathan's lame son, Mephibosheth, was the only remaining claimant to the throne and Saul's followers recognized that their cause was lost. David was a popular figure and they transferred their allegiance to him.

It seems likely that David continued to rule from Hebron for the next five years. Ishbosheth's death left David as the solitary focus for Israelite loyalty but Philistine control had to be broken before David could rule effectively over a united kingdom of Israel. Information about David's struggles with the Philistines is sparse. Perhaps his earlier service with them had won him many friends among them and so eased his task. The one real struggle that is recorded tells of a notable victory which David won in the valley of Rephaim. It is probable that the capture of Jerusalem really followed that victory and marked a decisive stage in the accomplishment of David's task. Jerusalem was a very strong fortress town in a valuable strategic position. Once David had occupied Jerusalem his position would be fairly secure.

David captures Jerusalem and makes it his capital (2 Sam. v. 6-9)

The account of the capture of Jerusalem is far from clear in the A.V. The Hebrew text, at this point, has clearly suffered

DAVID THE KING 85

badly during the long period when it was being copied by hand. It is hardly possible to tell now what the original meaning of the passage may have been. Probably the taunt of the Jebusites meant that the fortress was so strong that the blind and the lame were sufficient to secure its safety. The Hebrew text of v.8 is so perplexing that it defies translation. The reference to the watercourse suggests that David's men secured entrance to the city by way of the sloping tunnel which supplied the inhabitants with water.

David's move from Hebron to Jerusalem was a most important and statesmanlike step. It was not sufficient for him to establish his military position in face of the Philistines. He had also to establish his political position as the acknowledged ruler of all the tribes of Israel. It is evident from the Old Testament that there was no real sense of unity between Judah and the northern tribes. David's association with Judah was therefore a handicap to him in winning the wholehearted loyalty of the north. That difficulty would have been emphasized if he had attempted to rule over the northern tribes from the southern centre of Hebron. Had he transferred his headquarters to a northern town he might have offended his own tribe. Jerusalem lay at an important strategic point between north and south. It had no previous association with either side and its natural strength, as a hill fortress, made it an ideal capital. So David built his palace there and Jerusalem began to become the focal point of Israelite loyalty.

David makes Jerusalem the religious centre of the nation (2 Sam. vi. 17–19; vii. 1–17)

David took a further step which was equally important. The sacred Ark of the LORD was brought from Kiriath-jearim to Jerusalem and David planned to build a Temple in which it might be fittingly housed. In taking such a step David ensured that Jerusalem would become the focus of religious emotion also and he strengthened greatly the position of the city as the capital of a united nation. His motives in bringing the Ark into Jerusalem were doubtless genuinely religious, but his action had political results also. The Temple was not actually built in David's reign and three different reasons are given in the Bible as explanation of that fact (cf. 1 Kings v.3 and 1 Chron. xxii. 8 with 2 Sam. vii. 5f). It seems likely that David's preoccupation with military tasks was the historical cause but it was remembered of David that it was 'in his heart' to build the Temple (see 1 Kings viii. 18), and Nathan the prophet is recorded as giving David a message of divine approval and the assurance that his dynasty would be established for ever.

David's kindness to Jonathan's son (2 Sam. ix.)

2 Sam. lix. marks the opening of a section of the book which is generally regarded as the earliest example of continuous narrative in the Old Testament. It is also a fine example of colourful and dramatic story-telling. Apart from one or two small editorial additions it runs without interruption to the end of chapter twenty and it is thought to be completed in 1 Kings i–ii. It deals entirely with the personal affairs of the king and his family and with events at the king's court. Various guesses at its possible authorship have been made but there is no real evidence on the subject. It does seem, however, that it must have been written by someone with first-hand knowledge of the events described.

The first incident recorded in this section illustrates one of the most attractive features in David's character. David had not reached the throne by right of inheritance and Saul still had relatives alive who might have provided a rallying point for a rebellion. It was common enough, in those days, for eastern monarchs to secure their position by putting to death any possible rivals and it would not have been surprising if David had taken such a step. But David was a man of generous feelings and strong loyalties. He bore no malice himself and he was slow to suspect treachery in others. Jonathan had been his closest friend and David would have found it hard, indeed, to safeguard his own position by an act which stained the memory of that friendship. His generous attitude towards Mephibosheth may, indeed, have been partly due to David's own sorrowful associations with the circumstances in which

Mephibosheth had received the injury which had left him lame. His nurse had dropped Mephibosheth as she fled on

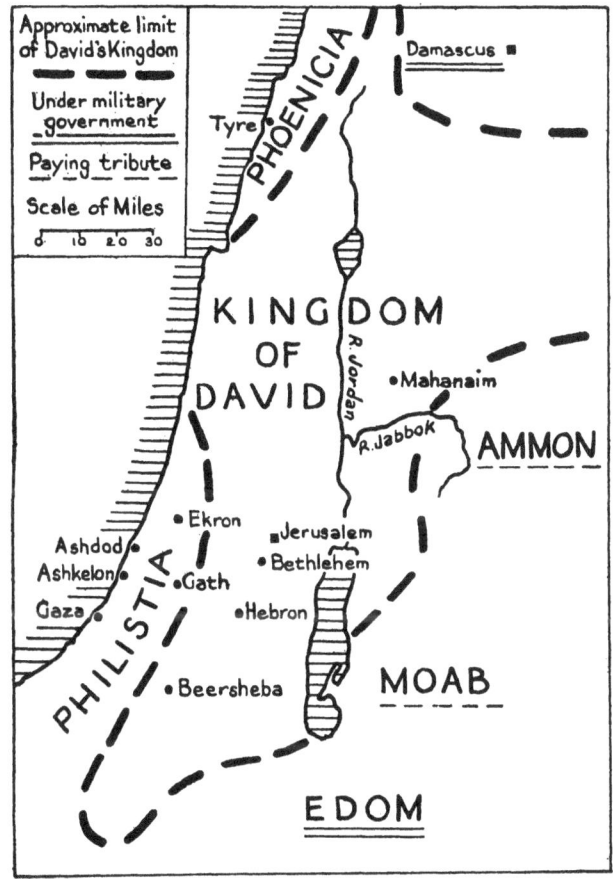

The kingdom of David

receiving news of the disastrous battle which had cost Saul and Jonathan their lives.

According to a passage in 2 Sam. xxi. David found himself

compelled, for political reasons, to allow the Gibeonites to revenge themselves on Saul's family for a treacherous act by their father. Seven of Saul's male descendants perished. It is possible that distress over this event provided the immediate motive for David's generosity to Mephibosheth. It may be that he was seeking a way of making amends. The account of his action certainly begins very abruptly and some scholars have suggested that it originally followed the story of his dealings with the Gibeonites.

Such a suggestion does not really affect the impression conveyed by the story. Any ordinary eastern monarch, in those days, might have been expected to welcome a good excuse for wiping out the descendants of his royal predecessor. The very fact that David had feelings of compunction would, in itself, illustrate his generous and sensitive nature. His treatment of Jonathan's son completes the picture. Saul's land and property had naturally been confiscated when David became king. They were now restored and Mephibosheth himself was brought to the palace and was treated like one of David's own sons.

David's treachery towards Uriah (2 Sam. xi. 1-4, 14-27)

David's emotional nature led him astray on more than one occasion. It sometimes clouded his judgement, as we shall see later, but on one occasion it silenced his conscience. David's treacherous dealings with Uriah, the husband of Bathsheba, is a dark blot on his character. An eastern king of that period would not have hesitated to take a new wife into his harem although he knew that she was already married to one of his subjects. A king's rights were supreme. His action might have been resented but it would not have been condemned. But David was no ordinary eastern king. He was the LORD'S anointed, and all Israel knew that kings, as well as their subjects, must live in accordance with the laws of the LORD. David was fully aware that he was acting wrongly and he tried to hide the consequences of his action.

David's secret instructions to Joab show how far his emotions had blinded his moral judgement. It was strangely callous and despicable that he should actually have used Uriah to carry the message which contained his own death sentence. David's plan was successful and Uriah was slain in battle. The way was clear for Bathsheba to be received openly into the king's palace before her child was born.

David is rebuked by Nathan (2 Sam. xii. 1–5)

Some scholars question whether the story of Nathan's intervention formed part of the original narrative. It is certainly true that the sequence of the story would be improved by removing it and it is possible that an editor added it from another source. There is no reason to doubt its genuineness, however, and it gives another typical picture illustrating the relationship between prophets and kings in Israel.

It is significant that Nathan's rebuke focuses on David's abuse of his royal power. The story of the rich man who took the precious ewe lamb from the poor man is obviously a story in which power and privilege are selfishly misused. David's offence had not stopped at adultery. He had not scrupled to use his royal authority to secure the death of the man who stood between him and the satisfaction of his selfish passions.

David's action seems mean and treacherous in our eyes. And so it was. But the very fact that David felt it necessary to get rid of Uriah before he took Bathsheba openly as his wife is a clear indication of the moral standards of contemporary society. He could not ignore the moral judgement of Israelite society and his own conscience condemned him when Nathan told his story. Nathan's intervention would not have been tolerated outside of Israel but David listened to Nathan's rebuke and acknowledged his own sin. This is not an idealized portrait painted by a pious historian of later times. We are dealing with a narrative which is generally regarded as a contemporary record of events and it is evident, therefore, that the whole incident shows very clearly how firmly rooted the moral traditions of Israel's religious faith were at this stage in the people's history.

David's foolish treatment of Absalom (2 Sam. xiv. 25-33)

The graphic story of Absalom's rebellion exposes another, more pardonable, weakness in David's character. His strong affections clouded his judgement in dealing with problems of family life. Absalom had been guilty of a brother's death and justice demanded punishment. But Absalom's action had been taken in revenge for a crime that had gone unpunished. David's affection for his eldest son had prevented him from punishing the elder brother and Absalom may well have felt resentful that punishment had fallen on him when the original offence had been condoned. It is possible that the seeds of Absalom's disloyalty were sown in these early years.

In his dealings with Absalom David showed clearly that warm personal affection for his son was at war with the claims of impersonal justice. He had banished Absalom because justice demanded punishment but he was quick to respond when Joab, his trusted commander-in-chief, pleaded for Absalom's pardon. If personal emotion had not been so deeply involved he might have pardoned Absalom completely and regained his full confidence and affection. It would seem, however, as if David felt that he must not allow his personal affections to overrule the claims of justice completely. He seems, indeed, to have done violence to his own feelings in the interests of justice. Although he allowed Absalom to return to Jerusalem he refused to see him for two years.

This vacillating conduct had its natural consequences. By drastic methods Absalom succeeded in prevailing on Joab to use his influence with the king again and a full reconciliation followed but Absalom used his restored position for his own selfish ends. He had all his father's strong feelings and personal charm but he could harbour resentment as David could not do and he had ruthless and unscrupulous ambitions. No doubt disappointment at the delay in receiving him back into full favour had increased whatever resentment he may already have felt towards his father. He was now the legitimate heir to the throne and he soon began to assume the dignities of that position and to seek popularity among his future subjects.

DAVID THE KING 91

Absalom plans a rebellion and seizes the throne (2 Sam. xv. 1-17)

The principal gateway of an eastern city was always an important centre of social life. In the shelter from the hot sun which the city wall provided, commercial and legal business was transacted and persons of importance were honoured by the populace. When Absalom was restored to the king's favour he began to frequent the city-gate of Jerusalem. Visitors from far and near came to the capital on business of many kinds. Among them there would always be some who had legal business to lay before the king. David was growing old and probably such business was not always dealt with very promptly. Absalom seized every opportunity to win the sympathy of dissatisfied subjects by flattery and fair words. In such ways he deceived the people and won a reputation throughout the nation for his friendly desire to help. The Bible says that 'he stole the hearts of the men of Israel', but in Hebrew idiom the heart was not, as it is with us, the seat of emotion. It was the centre of intellectual and moral judgement. No doubt Absalom did charm the hearts of the people, in our sense of that phrase, but the Bible means that he deprived them of their powers of judgement.

After four years of such behaviour Absalom apparently felt himself to be in a strong enough position to make an open bid for the throne. He sought permission from David to go to Hebron in order that he might sacrifice there in fulfilment of a vow made in exile. Perhaps he chose David's old capital as a centre for revolt because he knew that David's own tribesmen in the south were growing resentful of his increasing friendship with the northern tribes. We may be sure, at least, that Absalom's preparations were carefully made and that the 'spies' were merely warning his friends that the moment for open revolt had come. When Absalom reached Hebron, 'the sound of the trumpet' was heard and Absalom was hailed as king. The preparations had apparently been so thorough that there was at once a general rising in Absalom's favour. David was taken completely by surprise and he decided to seek refuge across the Jordan.

A foreigner's loyalty to David (2 Sam. xv. 18–23)

Two incidents occurred during David's flight which throw a significant light on his personal influence and on the depth and sincerity of his religious devotion. Among his immediate followers there was a Philistine from the town of Gath with a bodyguard of six hundred men. There is no indication whether this foreigner was a political exile who had attached himself to David's court or whether he was a mercenary soldier but his personal loyalty to David in this hour of disaster is very striking. It shows the man himself in a very favourable light but it also illustrates the warm personal loyalty which David awakened among his friends and followers. With typical generosity David wanted to release him from any obligations to a king who seemed to have lost his throne but Ittai swore that he would stand by David 'for death or for life'.

David sends back the Ark to Jerusalem (2 Sam. xv. 24–9)

David's attitude to the Ark of the LORD at this crisis in his fortunes is also very striking. When he left the city the priests in charge of the Ark assumed that it would go with him. In earlier days men had thought that the presence of the Ark with the armies of Israel was a guarantee that the LORD was with them and would give them victory (cf. Num. x. 35f; 1 Sam. iv. 3). Even in David's day it seemed important that the Ark should go with the king at such a critical time. But David thought differently. He was too conscious of his own failings to have any confidence in seeking divine aid. He was ready to accept humbly whatever God might have in store for him and he was apparently confident that the presence or absence of the Ark would not affect God's power to help him. Accordingly he sent back the two priests and their sons, with the Ark, to Jerusalem.

David's secret agent in Jerusalem (2 Sam. xv. 30–37; xvii. 1–16)

One further incident took place during David's flight which had important consequences. As David and his friends passed the sanctuary on the Mount of Olives one of his courtiers, Hushai the Archite, met him. David had already learned that

Ahithophel, another member of his court, had joined Absalom. He therefore urged Hushai to go back into Jerusalem and attach himself to Absalom so that he might work secretly against Ahithophel and might also keep David in touch with all that happened within the city. The sons of the priests in charge of the Ark were to act as secret messengers between Hushai and David.

This plan proved very fruitful. Hushai welcomed Absalom to Jerusalem and succeeded in finding acceptance among the king's advisors. Ahithophel was the grandfather of Bathsheba and he may have been moved by personal enmity towards David. At any rate he advised Absalom to pursue David at once and secure his death. Once David was dead, he argued, all fear of further strife would be over. Whatever Ahithophel's motives may have been the advice had obvious wisdom and Absalom was so utterly ruthless in pursuit of his ambition that he was ready to act upon it. But first he wanted to learn what Hushai had to say. This was Hushai's opportunity, and he stressed the possible dangers in Ahithophel's scheme. David's personal bravery was well known and the reputation of his bodyguard stood high. Hasty action, counselled Hushai, might be disastrous. It would be wiser to delay until a large army had been gathered which Absalom could lead in person. Hushai's advice was taken and he was able to warn David to prepare for a decisive battle.

The rebels are defeated and Absalom is slain (2 Sam. xviii.)

David had established himself with his followers, in Mahanaim, the chief city of Gilead. It lay to the north of the river Jabbok, on the east side of the Jordan. He had succeeded in gathering together a formidable army of followers and he made careful preparations for the coming struggle. His faithful general Joab was with him and divided the command with his brother Abishai and with Ittai, the Philistine from Gath, while David himself kept a detachment in reserve under his own command. One thing concerned the king above all else. Personal anxiety for the safety of his wayward but dearly-loved son was uppermost in his mind and he urged his commanders to 'deal gently' with Absalom. When the battle was joined the rebel army was heavily defeated and Absalom himself met a strange fate. While he was riding at high speed through the forest his mule passed under a large oak tree. Absalom's head was caught, and became wedged between two branches. He was swung off his mule and he hung suspended in the air. Joab was well aware of David's passionate concern for Absalom's safety but he felt that greater issues were at stake than a father's feelings. When he learned of Absalom's predicament he saw a chance of crushing finally the rebellion against David and, with his own hand, he stabbed Absalom in the heart.

David regains control of the kingdom (2 Sam. xix. 1–15)

The passage which tells how the tidings of Absalom's death were brought to David is most graphic and most moving. David's grief and his people's sympathy are described very beautifully. The triumphant joy of victory is turned in a moment to sympathetic sorrow. Joab alone seems to have recognized the danger that lay in David's attitude. Personal emotion was again clouding the king's judgement. Deep though his personal sorrow at Absalom's death might be, the need for action was urgent. Public duty must take precedence over private sorrow. A great military victory had been won but David's political position had yet to be restored. The unity of the kingdom was still in danger. David must show himself among his people and recapture their loyalty.

David recognized the truth of Joab's words and his qualities of statesmanship reasserted themselves. The death of Absalom had left the country leaderless and David's own achievements and qualities had not been forgotten. Recognizing that the rebellion had arisen among his own tribesmen David turned first to the leaders of Judah. Pointing out that the tide of opinion was already flowing strongly in his favour among the northern tribes he urged them, as his kinsmen, to take the initiative in recognizing him again as their king. They did so and sent messengers to bring David back across the Jordan. Thus the rebellion ended where it had begun and David's position became stronger than it had been before.

David's last instructions to Solomon (1 Kings ii. 1–11)

David's last instructions to Solomon his son and successor raise some difficult problems. His instructions regarding the sons of Barzillai are quite in character. Barzillai of Gilead had come to his aid in the days of Absalom's rebellion (see 2 Sam. xvii. 27–9; xix. 31–9) and David did not forget his friends. But the instructions regarding Joab and Shemei are in a different category. They seem to show David exhibiting a vindictiveness at the close of his life which is at variance with the general picture of his character. This difficulty has been felt so acutely that some scholars would suggest that the whole passage (1 Kings ii. 1–12) is the work of a later writer who tried to idealize Solomon by blaming David for some of the bloodshed which marked the beginning of Solomon's reign. Solomon certainly had good reason to fear the enmity of Shimei, whose sympathies had been with the house of Saul, and of Joab who had supported Solomon's rival in the struggle for succession to David. It is generally agreed that vv. 2–4 and vv. 10–12 have come from an editorial hand and it would certainly simplify matters if the whole passage could be regarded as unhistorical. On the other hand there is no real evidence to support that view and the passage as a whole is generally regarded as belonging to the same contemporary document as 2 Samuel ix.–xx.

David and Joab (1 Kings ii. 5–6)

It is not easy to explain David's instructions regarding his faithful general, Joab. Joab's crimes had not harmed David or his cause. Abner had been Saul's commander-in-chief and on Saul's death he had supported Saul's son Ishbosheth at first but he had entered later into negotiations with David. Joab distrusted Abner and he had personal reasons for taking vengeance on him, so he killed him treacherously. The death of their strong leader had led directly to the collapse of Ishbosheth and his followers so that David actually had gained by Abner's death. Amasa had been appointed commander-in-chief by David in place of Joab because of the latter's disobedience in slaying Absalom, but Amasa had proved too slow in an emergency (2 Sam. xx. 5) and again David's cause had been aided by Joab's treacherous violence. It is difficult to believe that David harboured resentment against Joab for the death of Absalom. The more likely explanation is that David remembered with dismay on his death-bed that he had allowed these crimes of violence to go unpunished. Justice seemed to demand that blood be paid for blood that had been spilled and David's personal loyalties and finer feelings were submerged by his superstitious reverence for the traditions of a more primitive age.

David and Shimei (1 Kings ii. 8-9)

The case of Shimei is even more difficult to excuse. Shimei was certainly a despicable character who had cursed the king in the day of his downfall and had hastened to seek reconciliation in the hour of his victory (see 2 Sam. xvi. 5-14; xix. 16-23). But David had refused to allow his followers to slay Shimei on either occasion. Indeed he had solemnly sworn to Shimei that he would not suffer death. It seems dishonourable in David to instruct Solomon to put to death a man whose life he himself had sworn to spare. It is possible that the explanation must again be sought in David's superstitious fears. Shimei had cursed him and when a curse was once uttered it remained potent unless it could be made to recoil on the head of him who uttered it. Possibly David was seeking a way of ensuring that this curse would have no power to harm him, or his descendant, without breaking the literal terms of his own oath sworn to Shimei.

David's achievements

David was not free from the moral limitations and the primitive superstitions of his age but he was undoubtedly a man of great gifts and qualities. By his military and political leadership he established an Israelite kingdom. By his own deep religious devotion he ensured that faith in the LORD, who

DAVID THE KING 97

had brought their ancestors out of Egypt, would become the established national religion of Israel. At the close of his reign the kingdom of Israel controlled the greatest stretch of territory in Palestine ever ruled by an Israelite king. If his successor had been a man of equal stature the power of Israel might have become a dominant influence among the great empires of the East. Had that happened, however, her religion might never have been set free from national limitations.

During David's reign the framework of national organization took shape and the old tribal divisions became less important. Jerusalem became the centre of national life and it attracted to itself the leading personalities in the kingdom. David had the beginnings of a standing army, which included mercenary elements, drawn from other nations, and its leaders played an important part in the life of the court. In 2 Sam. viii. 16–18 and xx. 23–6 there are lists of officials which show how the administrative life of the country was developing. The *recorder* and the *scribe* would be in charge of the official records of the kingdom and would be responsible for the growing volume of official correspondence. The controller of the *tribute* would be responsible for organizing labour gangs which gave compulsory unpaid labour as a form of taxation. The king himself was the ultimate authority in legal disputes but most of them would probably be solved locally in accordance with traditional practice. Tribal loyalties died slowly, however, and jealousy between the northern and the southern tribes showed itself on more than one occasion (2 Sam. xix. 40–3; xx.1–2). As a result of Solomon's tyrannical rule this antagonism gave rise to a disastrous division in the kingdom.

The ideal king of Israel's memories and hopes

A significant feature in David's reign is the covenant with which it opened (2 Sam. v. 3). With all his faults David was a true Israelite king and he became the ideal kingly figure of later tradition. He was not a typical eastern monarch. There were no limits to the power of an eastern king. His control over his subjects was absolute and it could be used to satisfy any personal whim or ambition. Among the Hebrews a different conception of the monarchy prevailed from the beginning. The rights of an Israelite king were limited by his responsibilities before the LORD, the God of Israel. The covenant was the expression of that conception. At his anointing the Israelite king entered into covenant with the LORD and with the people of the LORD. Not all Israelite kings seem to have pledged themselves openly in this way and few of them were faithful to the covenant. Nevertheless this covenant was always implicit in the Israelite idea of the monarchy and it was remembered of David that he had entered into the covenant and that he had been faithful to it.

Was David really a man after God's own heart? (See 1 Sam. xiii. 14.) In many respects his conduct and his outlook fall far short of the standard set before us in the New Testament. Judged against the background of his period, however, he was a man of such outstanding qualities of mind and character that he was naturally idealized by later generations. It must be remembered, too, that it was his leadership which established the Israelites in the land which, according to their religious traditions, had been promised to their fathers. Moses had brought their fathers out of Egypt but David was the leader in the golden age of their history. He was the ideal king through whom God's promises seemed, in part at least, to have been fulfilled. In later centuries of suffering and disappointment David's memory provided a focus for their most precious hopes. Confident that God had a high destiny in store for their people they looked for the coming of another David, a 'son of David', in whom these hopes would be fulfilled (cf. Isa. xi. 1–8; Ezek. xxxvii. 24f.).

CHAPTER 10

SOLOMON: BUILDER OF THE TEMPLE

A struggle for the throne (1 Kings i.)
Solomon reached the throne as the result of a palace intrigue. Adonijah was David's oldest surviving son, and he naturally regarded himself as the heir to the throne. No fixed principle of succession had yet been established, however, and the opening chapter of 1 Kings, shows the influence of three different ideas. Although the Bible traces the initial choice of Saul and David to divine selection through Samuel, it recognizes that both men were confirmed in office by popular acclamation (1 Sam. xi. 15; 2 Sam. v. 1–3). According to 1 Kings ii. 15 Adonijah had that popular support. He was thus in a strong position because the eldest son enjoyed the rights and privileges of leadership in the family according to traditional Hebrew custom (cf. stories of Jacob and Esau). He had two good reasons for regarding himself as David's legitimate heir. But it was also recognized that the reigning monarch had a right to nominate his successor (1 Kings i. 20, 27), and it was on that admission that the possibility of intrigue was based.

Adonijah assumed the dignity of an heir apparent during his father's lifetime. He secured for himself a bodyguard of chariots and horsemen, just as Absalom had done (cf. 1 Kings i. 5 with 2 Sam. xv. 1). All who saw him travelling in this royal style would recognize that he was regarding himself as David's heir. His father's faithful commander-in-chief, Joab, and Abiathar the priest, who had also shown himself to be a loyal friend of David, sympathized with Adonijah's aspirations and made plans to have him officially proclaimed as king. But there were other influential figures who were opposed to Adonijah. Among them was Nathan, the prophet, and he took the initiative by approaching Bathsheba, the mother of Solomon. No motive is given for his action but it is possible that he knew that David favoured Solomon and he may have approved of the king's choice. Adonijah's plan for securing the throne was forestalled by Bathsheba and Nathan. David confirmed his personal choice of Solomon and he gave orders that Solomon should be anointed immediately as joint ruler and successor.

The record of Solomon's reign

The Biblical record of Solomon's reign does not give us any consecutive narrative and it does not preserve a chronological order. It seems to have been put together in a somewhat haphazard manner from three main sources. Official court and Temple records account for two of these and the third is named in 1 Kings ii. 41; 'the book of the Acts of Solomon'. The last-named document seems to have consisted mainly of biographical narrative. There are also some important, late, editorial additions such as the prayer of dedication at the opening of the Temple (1 Kings viii. 22–53). The editors seem to have been influenced by two motives in selecting and putting together their material. They have used material which emphasized Solomon's wisdom and royal splendour, and they have focused attention also on his achievements in the planning and building of Israel's first national Temple.

The character of Solomon's reign

There can be no doubt that the Old Testament portrait of Solomon is idealized and exaggerated. The fact that he built the Temple gave him a special place in the religious traditions of a people for whom the Temple had such sacred associations. The oriental splendour of his reign doubtless left an afterglow in his people's memories during later years of division and decline so that his achievements tended to be magnified and his weaknesses were forgotten. But no careful reader of the Bible story can miss the indications which point to the truth. Solomon inherited a kingdom which had been established and consolidated by his father's military skill and political wisdom. His extravagant and oppressive rule left that kingdom ripe for rebellion.

SOLOMON: BUILDER OF THE TEMPLE 101

Solomon was certainly able and ambitious. He saw and seized the opportunities for foreign trade, which lay in Israel's geographical position. He had wide interests and he brought his people into a larger world of political and cultural life. But his interests and ambitions were largely self-centred. His people may have enjoyed basking in the reflected glories of his royal splendour, but they seem to have given Solomon no real place in their affections. Solomon may have been admired but he was not loved.

The wisdom of Solomon (1 Kings iii.)

The stories that a people remember and tell about great men of the past generally tell us a good deal about the personalities of the men. David was remembered as the youth who killed the Philistine champion—and that story commemorated David's bravery and his military achievements—but it was also remembered of him that he was chosen of God for his high office. The story of Samuel rejecting each of David's older brothers, against his own judgement and in response to divine prompting, emphasizes the fact that David was remembered, above all, for his moral and religious qualities and leadership.

In Solomon's case the parallel story is the story of his dream. When Solomon succeeded to the throne he celebrated the occasion by a solemn and impressive sacrificial service. No doubt the occasion would stir all that was best in Solomon and his dream, if it is historical, may have expressed the stirrings of generous ideals. It certainly expressed a fine appreciation of the responsibilities which lay before him as David's successor. Does the promise of riches and honour given in the dream betray the divided loyalties in Solomon's secret soul? Was it the voice of God, or the voice of his own unconscious desires which spoke that promise? The latter view would certainly make the dream a fitting introduction to, and comment on, the reign of David's successor. He was a man who had been endowed with great intellectual gifts, but his deep love of personal luxury and splendour distorted his use of these gifts as ruler of Israel.

It is certainly significant that this dream should be prominent in the Old Testament account of Solomon's reign. This is the story which marks God's recognition of Solomon's accession. There is no mention of divine selection and the qualities which are commemorated are intellectual rather than moral, or religious. That fact is brought out very clearly in the story which follows the dream and which is obviously intended to illustrate Solomon's gift of wisdom. We might regard the incident as illustrating astute cleverness rather than real wisdom.

Solomon's wisdom is also commemorated by his traditional association with the book of Proverbs (see also 1 Kings iv. 32). It is again significant that he should be associated with that book while his father David is associated with the book of Psalms. Neither David nor Solomon was responsible, of course, for composing all the material in the two books associated with them. Each book is an anthology, and each contains material of differing date and authorship. Some of the psalms may have been composed by David and some of the wise sayings in the book of Proverbs may have originated with Solomon. Most of the material in both books belongs undoubtedly to a later age than either David or Solomon. Yet the traditional association remains important and significant. The religious poetry of the book of Psalms is fittingly associated with David and the wise sayings of the book of Proverbs are appropriately linked with the name of Solomon. The popular wisdom of the book of Proverbs is not particularly Jewish. And Solomon had wide contacts outside of his own nation. Many of the wise sayings, too, have a shrewd, worldly flavour and little religious depth. The difference between the book of Psalms and the book of Proverbs illustrates very clearly the differing impression which David and Solomon left on their people's memory.

Solomon's contacts with Egypt (1 Kings iii. 1)

The account of Solomon's marriage to an Egyptian Princess, draws attention to his contacts with that country. Such a marriage generally implies a political alliance and, when the

SOLOMON: BUILDER OF THE TEMPLE   103

wife comes from a much more powerful country, it can generally be assumed that the superior position is being recognized by the weaker country. It would look, therefore, as if the Pharaoh of Egypt had taken Solomon and the kingdom of Israel under his friendly protection at this point. It is interesting to notice that Egypt already possessed a rich store of popular wisdom of the kind that we find in the book of Proverbs. The collection called the *Wisdom of Amenemope* was probably in existence at this time and some passages in Proverbs are so similar that they must have been derived from it. Perhaps Solomon himself was familiar with Egyptian wisdom and began to collect and translate some of it.

We cannot tell which Pharaoh it was whose daughter was married to Solomon but it seems, from the Old Testament record, that he must have had more military power than most of the Pharaohs of that period. He is said to have captured the Canaanite town of Gezer and given it to Solomon as a dowry for his wife (1 Kings ix. 16). Gezer lies on the coastal slopes of the hills which guard the western approach to Jerusalem. It seems to have remained in the hands of the Canaanites until this time (see Judges i. 29), and there is archaeological evidence of destruction and rebuilding in this period. We know that Sheshonk, the founder of the twenty-second Egyptian dynasty, befriended a rebel during Solomon's life (1 Kings xi. 40), and led an army against Solomon's son (1 Kings xiv. 25). The friendship between Solomon and Egypt must, therefore, belong to the last years of the twenty-first dynasty.

An exaggerated picture of Solomon's power and dominions
(1 Kings iv. 20-34)

1 Kings iv. 20f., 24f., 29-34 are generally regarded as late additions to the book of Kings. They give a highly coloured picture of Solomon's widespread dominion which is not consistent with facts recorded elsewhere (e.g. 1 Kings xi. 14, 23). It was during David's reign that the territories of Israel reached their greatest extent. Edom and the area around Damascus, as well as Moab and Ammon, paid tribute to him

and his authority was recognized 'from Dan to Beersheba' (2 Sam. xxiv. 2). But during Solomon's reign Damascus and Edom asserted their independence. These verses added to chapter four by a late editor exaggerate Solomon's political power and, in similar vein, they magnify his wisdom and knowledge and make him a figure of world renown.

The cost of Solomon's grandeur (1 Kings iv. 22-3, 26-8)

The price which had to be paid for the regal splendour of Solomon's court is illustrated in 1 Kings iv. 22f., 26f. David had apparently adopted the use of war chariots from the Syrians (2 Sam. viii. 4) and Solomon seems to have extended this practice greatly. 1 Kings x. 26, 28f. gives us further information about the number and source of his chariots and horses. Archaeological excavation at Megiddo, which was rebuilt by Solomon (1 Kings ix. 15) has uncovered extensive stables, some of which probably go back to Solomon's own day. The purchase of these chariots and horses would be a heavy drain on the national purse and it is suspected that Solomon may have sold slaves to Egypt in payment. The scale of the daily rations for the royal household, and for the innumerable officials and workmen engaged in his ambitious building projects, gives a further indication of the enormous extent to which national spending must have grown in Solomon's day.

Solomon's building activities (1 Kings v., vi. 38; vii. 1, 51)

The building of the Temple was, of course, an important part of Solomon's building activities, although it bulks more largely in the Bible story than the facts probably warrant. The Bible writers were particularly interested in this enterprise and described it in considerable detail but it is worth noting, that even the Bible records that seven years were spent on the building of the Temple while it took thirteen to build Solomon's palace at Jerusalem (cf. 1 Kings vi. 38 and vii. 1). And Solomon also built, or rebuilt, many cities (1 Kings ix. 15-19).

Hiram, king of Tyre, had been a friend and ally of David (2 Sam. v. 11), and it was natural that he should send mes-

SOLOMON: BUILDER OF THE TEMPLE 105

sages of congratulation to Solomon when he came to the throne. It was equally natural that Solomon should use this opportunity to enter into negotiations with Hiram for the purchase of timber and for the supply of skilled workmen. Hiram had helped his father in that way, and he seems to have had control of the territory of Lebanon. The forests of Lebanon were rich in timber and provided a natural source for Solomon's building plans. The cost of the timber and of the labour, was to be met by an annual payment in wheat and oil.

Large numbers of Israelite workmen were also required to share in the cutting and transporting of the timber. Others were needed to quarry out limestone from the hills of Palestine. The necessary labour was raised by compulsory levy on Israelite manpower. Those who went to Lebanon spent one month there for every two months that they spent at home (1 Kings v. 14). Such a demand must have involved a good deal of hardship in a society which was largely composed of peasant farmers. Four months of forced labour away from the family land was a heavy demand.

The system of forced labour (1 Kings v. 13; ix. 15–23)

These labour levies were apparently a familiar feature of Solomon's reign (1 Kings ix. 15–23). It is said that he only imposed this levy on the Canaanite elements in the population but that statement is not very convincing. It is difficult to believe that the distinction between Canaanite and Israelite was at all clearly marked, in most areas, by Solomon's day. Moreover an earlier reference (1 Kings v. 13) explicitly mentions an Israelite levy. There is some evidence that Solomon's own tribal area may not have been included in the levy. It is thought likely that the twelve districts named in 1 Kings iv. 8–20 may have supplied labour levies, as well as food for the royal household, and it is noticeable that Judah does not figure in these lists. Such favoured treatment would help to account for the restiveness shown by the population of the north during Solomon's reign and for their revolt at the accession of his son Rehoboam.

The dedication of the Temple (1 Kings viii.)
The chapter which tells of the installation of the Ark of the LORD in the Temple and of the dedication of the Temple itself is full of interest and importance. Scholars consider it likely that the substance of vv. 1-13, together with verses 62-6, represent an early and reliable account of that event. The words attributed to Solomon in vv. 12f. seem to be an incomplete version of a poetic utterance which may actually have been spoken by Solomon. The Greek text of this chapter contains an additional introductory line which reads: 'He set the sun in the heavens'. If we add that to the words translated in the A.V., we get a four-lined stanza which expresses the belief that the LORD who set the sun in the heavens will dwell in the dark inner sanctuary of the Temple. The words seem appropriate to Solomon's period. They express the early belief that God Himself did dwell in the Holy of Holies within the Temple and, at the same time, they convey that sense of mystery and wonder which is so characteristic of Old Testament religion. vv. 10f. also express, in characteristic symbols (cf. Exod. xiii. 22; xxxiii. 9f.), the conviction that the LORD Himself had entered into His dwelling-place when the Ark was deposited within the Temple.

The address and prayer attributed to Solomon in vv. 14-61, probably belong to a much later date. It was a common practice for early historians to compose utterances expressing appropriate sentiments and attribute them to their leading characters on notable occasions. This was a very notable occasion in the eyes of Old Testament historians and it is not surprising that we should find three long utterances attributed to Solomon which seem, in language and thought, to belong to a later age. The early part of the prayer is particularly impressive but v. 27 clearly belongs to a later stage in religious thought than v. 13. In v. 13 God's presence in the Temple seems to be almost a physical presence but v. 27 recognizes that no earthly Temple can contain the infinite creator. It is already pointing forward to that fully spiritual understanding of religious worship which we find in the New Testament saying: 'God is Spirit: and they that worship

SOLOMON: BUILDER OF THE TEMPLE 107

Him must worship in spirit and truth' (John iv. 24, R.V.).

The Queen of Sheba visits Solomon (1 Kings x. 1–13)

The story of the Queen of Sheba's visit is doubtless intended to illustrate the reputation which Solomon had acquired in the world of his day. Sheba lay in the south-west of Arabia, and was known in later centuries as the centre of a great commercial empire. It is probable that the visit of the Queen was really connected originally with trading relationships. The visit of an important foreign queen, with an imposing display of splendour, would be striking evidence to the Israelites of the notable place which their king was winning for them among the nations of the earth. The visit would be much discussed and, in course of time, would be used to illustrate and to glorify Solomon's status and reputation. Later generations would remember with pride, that even the Queen of Sheba was quite overwhelmed by wonder at Solomon's grandeur and wisdom. It is evident that the story, as it has come down to us, is no longer a historical narrative. It is a story told to glorify the memory of Solomon's wisdom and royal splendour.

Solomon's trading activities (1 Kings x. 14–29)

There are important references to Solomon's commercial enterprises, in this same chapter, which help to explain the great increase of wealth which seems to have taken place during Solomon's reign. David's victories had given the Israelites control of important trade routes to the south and east and Solomon made good use of the opportunities which were thus open to him. He was able to levy customs dues on goods passing through territory controlled by Israel and he was able to engage in trade on his own account. He built up a merchant navy with the help of the experienced Phoenicians (1 Kings xi. 26–8; x. 22), and his ships made long journeys to purchase strange and precious merchandize in distant lands. There is no certainty about the route of Solomon's ships. Ophir is generally believed to have lain in Eastern Arabia on the shore of the Persian Gulf. No doubt the ships called at African ports on their way and some may even have visited India.

Ezion-geber was the harbour from which Solomon's ships set sail, and archaeological discoveries there have thrown further light on Solomon's commercial activities. The ancient port lies at the head of the Gulf of Akaba and the town was apparently planned as an industrial, as well as a seaport, town. There are valuable mineral deposits between the Gulf of Akaba and the Dead Sea, which were known and worked long before the days of Solomon. Important industrial plants have been discovered in Ezion-geber itself which seem to have been used for refining copper and iron ore, and for manufacturing metal objects. It seems evident from these discoveries that Solomon must have been responsible for notable developments in the mining and metal refining industries of that area. Much wealth may have come to the royal purse from these sources.

Solomon's extravagance (1 Kings x. 16-21)

It is evident, however, that Solomon's capacity to spend money was even greater than his gift for acquiring it. The references to the use of gold and ivory in the royal palace are no mere exaggeration. There can be little doubt that Solomon lived in luxury and magnificence and the record of his building projects is sufficient to show how freely money was spent throughout the country. After twenty years of building activity the royal exchequer was so impoverished that Solomon had apparently to give twenty towns in the region of Galilee to Hiram of Tyre in order to secure enough gold to pay his mounting debts (1 Kings ix. 10-14).

Solomon's moral and religious failure (1 Kings xi. 1-13)

The Old Testament historian, who gives such an impressive picture of Solomon's wisdom and splendour, draws attention at the end of his story to Solomon's religious failings and to some of the political troubles which developed in the course of his reign. A large harem was a normal aspect of oriental splendour. Solomon is credited with having many foreign wives in his harem and this inevitably created a religious problem. The foreign wives had to be given facilities for carrying on their familiar forms of worship. It is said by the historian that, in his old age, Solomon began to adopt the pagan practices of his foreign wives. The division of the kingdom after Solomon's death is regarded by him as a divine punishment for this lapse into paganism.

It may be questioned whether, in actual fact, Solomon was ever a true worshipper of the God of Israel. All that we know of his reign suggests that he was a selfish ambitious ruler who had little thought for the welfare of his subjects. Solomon's real apostasy was not the adoption of pagan religious practices. It was an apostasy of the heart and will. His heart was set on the fulfilment of his plans for national and personal glory, and his will was not dedicated to the purposes of God. The real 'punishment' of Solomon's failures came in the inevitable consequences of his selfish and oppressive rule.

The record of Solomon's reign gives no account of any ceremony of anointing nor does it speak of any solemn covenant between the king and the people. Solomon did not act as a king who was conscious of being set apart by the LORD to his high office. He showed no evidence of recognizing that he was in covenant with the LORD, and with the people of the LORD. It looks, indeed, as if the passage in Deut. xvii. 14–20, which gives the prophets' picture of a true Israelite king, had been written in the light of Solomon's failings. When it describes the way in which an Israelite king must not behave (vv. 16f.) it seems to be describing Solomon himself. And it certainly could not be said of Solomon that his heart was not 'lifted up above his brethren'.

A threat of revolt (1 Kings xi. 26-40)

A prophet figures only once in the records of Solomon's reign and on that occasion he is inciting rebellion. The story of this attempt at revolt during Solomon's lifetime (1 Kings xi. 26–40), throws a revealing light on the weaknesses of his rule and helps to explain the split in the kingdom which occurred when Rehoboam refused to repudiate his father's tyrannous ways (1 Kings xii. 1–20). The story is told more fully in the Greek version of the chapter and comparison of the two versions makes the probable development of events much clearer. Jeroboam belonged to Ephraim, a district in the northern territory of Israel, and he won favour with the king through notable service in restoring the fortifications of Jerusalem. He was appointed as overseer of forced labour gangs in his own home district. Possibly he sympathized with the Ephraimites when he realized the hardships caused by forced labour. The Greek version tells us that he raised a force of three hundred chariots and rebelled against Solomon. The rebellion was fruitless and he had to flee to Egypt, but it was this same Jeroboam who became king of the northern tribes on Solomon's death.

This story should be read along with the account of the petition brought by the deputation which came before Rehoboam on his accession to the throne. It was a plea for the lightening of their load of taxation and forced labour. When Rehoboam refused their plea and sent his chief labour overseer to deal with the revolt, the people stoned the overseer to death in their anger (1 Kings xii. 18). Jeroboam's attempted revolt was possible because the burden of taxation and forced labour was arousing discontent even during Solomon's lifetime. The division of the kingdom on Solomon's death was the direct result of his selfish tyranny.

The account of Ahijah's encouragement to Jeroboam deserves attention (1 Kings xi. 29–31, 40). It is another instance of the way in which Hebrew prophets made their influence felt by word or action, whenever they felt that moral and religious issues were at stake. Solomon had offended against the high tradition of the Israelite monarchy and Ahijah was ready to encourage the northern tribes to revolt against the policy and person of David's unworthy son. Solomon's reign had seen great advances in Israelite wealth and culture but he had ignored the fundamental needs of a healthy society. In the eyes of the prophet his reign had deserved, and would inevitably experience, the judgement of the LORD, the God of Israel.

EPILOGUE

DOES THE STORY REVEAL A PURPOSE?

Some awkward questions
The early books of the Old Testament raise many questions in the mind of an intelligent reader. There is the problem of the relation between historical fact and Biblical record. Did God really promise Abraham that his descendants would be a source of blessing to all mankind? Was there a real pillar of cloud and fire by which God guided the Israelites in the desert? An attempt has been made to deal with such questions at suitable points in the text. In the later stories a different problem arises. The books of Samuel and Kings tell us of actual historical events, but what do they teach us about God? How can stories of court intrigue and political revolt tell us anything of the nature and purpose of God? Where can we trace God's revelation of His purpose in the earlier books of the Old Testament?

God reveals Himself through events and men
We shall certainly not find divine revelation *primarily* in the actual narratives. God's revelation to the people of Israel was not given in a dictated book. God became known to Israel through great events in their history. These events were not necessarily 'supernatural' in the popular, though misleading, sense of that word. They were not necessarily events for which we today could find no intelligible explanation. They did not even compel belief among those who witnessed them. Neither the Egyptians nor the inhabitants of Jericho became worshippers of the LORD. And the tribes of Israel had many doubts and misgivings. The revelation was not given in the events alone. It was given through men to whom these events were full of meaning, and who declared the meaning of them to their contemporaries. These 'prophets',

as we call them, do not figure prominently in the historical books of the Old Testament but it was through their lives and teaching that the knowledge of God grew and deepened.

Moses

The great event from which the faith of Israel began was the escape from Egypt and the first great figure of prophetic stature was Moses. We have no contemporary record of Moses' life and teaching. We cannot be certain what parts of the traditional 'Laws of Moses' really originated with him. But it is quite clear from the facts of Israel's later history and religious development that he was the human founder of their faith. It was he who taught them to worship and serve the LORD who had brought them out of the land of Egypt.

Joshua

Joshua could hardly be regarded as a prophet. He was a military leader and he played a notable part in the story of his people. All that we know of him suggests that he was a genuinely religious man, although his outlook and actions were limited by the times in which he lived. It is likely that he did give important religious leadership also. It may have been through his influence that the faith of the desert tribes became the common traditions of the whole Israelite people (see Joshua xxiv. and p. 58). The book of Joshua opens with words of encouragement and exhortation: 'Be strong and of a good courage; be not afraid, neither be thou dismayed for the LORD thy God is with thee whithersoever thou goest'. It closes with a stirring call to religious decision: 'Choose ye this day whom ye will serve'. These opening and closing passages have religious teaching for all ages. They speak to us as they have spoken to men all through the centuries since the days of Joshua himself. But Christians read much fuller meaning into them than could have been present to the mind of Joshua. He was a faithful disciple of Moses, and a loyal servant of the LORD. But he was not a man of prophetic stature. He summoned men to loyalty to the traditions they had inherited from Moses' teaching but, as far as we can tell, he did not give the creative religious leadership of one who has received new and deeper insight from God Himself.

Samuel

The next figure of prophetic stature whom we meet is Samuel. The accounts of him are conflicting, and it is difficult to say whether he was a man of national or local significance. It is clear, however, that the Old Testament writers do not go astray when they say that in this time of crisis the word of the LORD 'came to Samuel'. It was out of a religious awakening that the impulse towards national unity came and all the evidence suggests that Samuel played a leading part in that awakening. He spoke and he acted under the constraint of an over-mastering conviction that God had called him and was guiding him.

Saul and David

Saul and David were not prophets in the true sense of the term. We are told that Saul was subject to periods of religious excitement, such as were typical of the prophet bands of his day (see 1 Sam. x. 10; xi. 6 and p. 77). But his later attacks of melancholia show the dangers in this unbalanced type of religious experience. David was a man of genuine religious devotion and he played a very important part in the religious history of his people. It was due to his influence, in large measure, that the religious faith brought from the desert became the established religion of the new Israelite kingdom. But there is no real evidence that deeper insight into God's nature and purpose came through David's leadership. The twenty-third psalm has led countless men and women closer to God. If we knew that David had written that psalm, and if we could identify other psalms which he had written, we should be compelled to recognize that his personal religious devotion had been a source of rich inspiration to all later generations. But even then we could hardly call him a prophet. Saul and David were outstanding leaders of men. They were, each in his own degree, worshippers of the God of Israel. We may learn from their achievements and we may find warning in their failures, but there is no evidence that fuller knowledge of God's purposes came through them.

Nathan and Ahijah

We hear little about the prophets during the reigns of David and Solomon. There do not seem to have been any men of outstanding prophetic stature at that time. Nevertheless the creative impulse was still active within Israelite society. We read of Nathan's rebuke to David and we have the story of Ahijah provoking a political revolt. There may have been no new insight given to these men but they showed creative religious leadership in their readiness to speak and to act under a sense of divine compulsion when selfish interests might have counselled them to be silent. They provide a not unworthy link in the succession which passes through Elijah and Elisha to the great prophets of the eighth, seventh and sixth centuries, whose teaching has been preserved within the books which bear their name.

The stories of the patriarchs

The history of the earlier centuries was written by men who had absorbed much of the teaching of these later prophets. The result is that the actual narratives of Old Testament history often contain moral and religious teaching which belongs to a much later period. In that secondary sense there is a revelation of God's nature and purpose which comes to us through the earlier books of the Old Testament. The stories of Abraham, Jacob and Joseph illustrate this fact very clearly.

It may well be true that there were ancestors of the Israelites in early times, like Abraham and Jacob, who were sensitive and responsive to the divine spirit. It would be foolish to insist that the revelation of God to the people of Israel only began with Moses. Nevertheless we cannot be sure what Abraham really knew of the nature and purpose of God. It is quite certain that the stories of the patriarchs introduce moral and religious ideas which belong to the period when they were being written down.

The historical narratives

The same difficulty faces us in the account of the Exodus, the travels in the desert, the settlement in Canaan and the story of the early monarchy. The history of all these events is read by us, through the spectacles of religious faith provided by writers of a later generation. When we come to the stories of David and Solomon we are reading records which are partly based on contemporary documents. The historical detail is much fuller and more reliable. Much of it is of great literary and historical interest. But the general point of view from which it is presented is still the religious viewpoint of a later age. It is therefore very difficult indeed to distinguish between the insights into God's nature and purpose which had already been received in the period when the incidents took place and the insights which are derived from a later age.

A living and growing faith

It does seem clear, however, that from the days of Moses, at least, the faith of Israel contained the seeds of those central truths which came to full fruition in the New Testament. The experience of deliverance, the challenge to moral obedience and the promise of 'salvation' were all part of that covenant relationship which began with Moses. The deliverance of which the early Israelites were conscious was a national and physical deliverance. The salvation for which they looked was a national and material salvation. The obedience which they believed they owed to God, included cruel slaughter and sacrifice. But the faith of Israel was a faith capable of growth because it was Israel's response to God's revelation of Himself. The Israelites—when they were true to the prophetic traditions —did not try to use God for their own ends. The pagan worshippers of ancient Canaan tried to compel the powers of the unseen world to grant them their desires. Semi-pagan Christians still try to do the same thing. But the great prophets of Israel were men who had learned to surrender self to the claims of God. Because they had done so they were able to see more clearly what God's nature and purpose was, and to point their people forward towards fuller understanding.

The religious education of a people

Hosea used the parent-child relationship to describe God's dealings with Israel (cf. Hos. xi. 1-4), and that is a useful metaphor to guide us in our thinking about God's earlier revelation of His purpose. The Old Testament describes the religious education of a people who knew that they had been called to be, in a special sense, the children of God. In the period from Abraham to Solomon we are still dealing with the childhood, and early adolescence of God's people Israel. We need not be surprised, therefore, if we meet much that is crude and ugly in their story and if we find it hard at times to recognize the origins of that religious faith which we meet in its full perfection in the New Testament. The men of the Old Testament are our spiritual ancestors and we can learn from them all—from Saul and David as well as from Moses and Samuel. But they were only beginning to learn of God's ways, and to walk in His paths (Isa. ii. 3). We can see a great deal in their character and conduct which we must repudiate for we have Jesus Christ as our supreme leader and teacher. But they had set their feet on that same way of faith, of which he became 'the pioneer and perfecter' (Heb. xii. 2, R.S.V.).

SOME QUESTIONS

ABRAHAM

1. Write a character sketch of Abraham, based on the story of his migration from Haran and his relationships with Lot, Ishmael and Isaac.
2. Find out all you can about the ancient cities of Ur and Haran. Describe the life with which Abraham must have been familiar as a boy.
3. Did Abraham act rightly or wrongly when he set out with Isaac to offer him as a sacrifice to God?
4. How can we be sure that God is really speaking to us?

JACOB

1. Write an essay comparing the characters of Jacob and Esau and showing the good and bad qualities in each.
2. What did Jacob learn from his dream at Bethel?
3. Why was Jacob a better heir to the promises of God than Esau?
4. Describe Jacob's experience at the river Jabbok and discuss its meaning.

JOSEPH

1. Describe the changes in Jacob's experience from his boyhood in Canaan to the time when he became ruler of Egypt under Pharaoh: what differences can you trace in his character during that same period?
2. What were Joseph's motives in accusing Benjamin of stealing the silver cup? Was he acting fairly?
3. 'So now it was not you that sent me hither but God'. (Gen. xlv. 8*a*). Do you agree with Joseph?
4. Read Rom. viii. 28, in a modern translation: what does it teach us about the Christian doctrine of providence? Do Christians never suffer misfortune?

5. Make a sketch map of Mesopotamia, Palestine and northern Egypt; trace on it the movements of Abraham, Jacob and Joseph.

MOSES

1. Make a sketch map tracing the route which, in your judgement, the Israelites took when they left Egypt and travelled to Mt Sinai.
2. Write a character sketch of Moses and show how his character developed.
3. What do you think Moses learned about the nature of God through his experience at Mt Horeb?
4. Was the crossing of the Red Sea a miracle? What is a miracle?

JOSHUA

1. Is the evidence of the archaeologist a help, or a hindrance, to us in our study of the Bible?
2. What can we expect the archaeologist to prove and what can he not prove?
3. Read Joshua xxiv. and separate out the three types of religious loyalty which Joshua put before the people at Shechem.
4. What qualities of character can you trace in the stories of Joshua's leadership?

SAMUEL

1. Read 1 Sam. vii. 5-17 and viii, note what is said about (i) the Philistine danger, (ii) Samuel's position in the land, (iii) the reasons given by the people in asking for a king. Compare the information given on these same points in 1 Sam. ix. 5-14 and 1 Sam. ix. 16.
2. Read 1 Sam. xv. carefully and consider what Saul's motives may have been in sparing Agag and the best of the animals. Indicate the evidence for your conclusions.
3. Find a sentence in the Gospels which might be quoted in defence of Samuel's condemnation of Saul and another

SOME QUESTIONS 119

which shows clearly that Samuel had still much to learn about God.

DAVID THE WARRIOR

1. Pick out the verses in the story of David and Goliath which show David's trust in God.
2. Write a short essay on the friendship of David and Jonathan, illustrating your description by reference to incidents in the Bible story.
3. Saul and David were both religious men: describe and discuss the different ways in which religious faith showed itself in the character of the two men. Would you agree with the view that David was religious but Saul was superstitious?
4. Was David acting disloyally by serving in the Philistine army?

DAVID THE KING

1. Write a character sketch of David, showing the strength and weakness that marked his reign.
2. Give an account of Absalom's rebellion; discuss Absalom's motives in rebelling: show why the rebellion succeeded and how it was overthrown.
3. Why was David's capture of Jerusalem a very important step in the establishment of the Israelite kingdom?
4. Do you think that David deserves to be called a man 'after God's own heart'?

SOLOMON

1. Describe the good and bad points in Solomon's reign. Does he deserve his reputation for wisdom?
2. How do you account for the Biblical emphasis on Solomon's wisdom?
3. Why did a prophet encourage revolt against King Solomon?
4. Draw a sketch map showing the probable route of Solomon's ships: mark the probable sources of their cargo.

GENERAL QUESTIONS
1. How does God speak to men?
2. Did God reveal Himself more clearly through David or through Nathan?
3. Can we learn more of God from the Old Testament than from the religious teaching of Buddhism or from the great religious literature of India?
4. What can we learn of God from the stories of Saul, David and Solomon?

INDEX

Abner, 95f.
Acts of Solomon, 100
Adam, 53f.
Adonijah, 99
Adullam, Cave of, 78f.
Aegean civilization, 63
Ahijah, 110
Ahithophel, 93
'Ain Qedeis, 47
Akaba, Gulf of, 35, 43f., 108
Amalekites, 71f., 77, 82
Ammon, Ammonites, 11, 103
Archaeology: Nuzu tablets, 4, 11
  Ur and Haran, 6
  Date of Exodus, 35f.
  Fall of Jericho, 54–6
  Conquest of Ai, 57f.
  Capture of Gezer, 103
  Solomon's stables, 104
  Ezion-geber, 108
Ashtaroth, 63
Ark of the LORD, 53, 85, 92

Baalim, 63
Barzillai, 95
Bathsheba, 88f., 99
Beersheba, 18f., 104
Bethel, 18f., 23, 56
Bethlehem, 78f., 82
Book of Jasher, 82

Canaan, 5, 30, 32, 56f., 59, 62
Canaanites, 58, 62f.
Child sacrifice, 12f.
City-gate, 91
'Coat of many colours', 28f.
Covenant: Sinai, 48
  Shechem, 58f.
  Israelite kings, 97, 109

Divine revelation, 7f., 38f., 46f., 67, 111–6
Dreams in the Old Testament, 18f., 27f., 101f.

Edom, Edomites, 3, 14, 103
Eliezer, 4, 10

Ephod, 69
Ezion-geber, 108

Fertility cults, 59, 63
Fire, smoke, cloud and the divine presence, 11, 38, 43, 50
Forced labour, 97, 105, 110
Freud, 36

Garstang, 55
Gath, 82, 92f.
Gibeah, 78
Gibeonites, 88
Gilgal, 54
Goshen, 25, 32, 41

Hagar, 11
Haran, 5, 18, 21, 23, 26f.
Hebrew names and their meaning, 15f., 22f.
Hebron 82, 84f., 91
Hiram of Tyre, 103f., 108
Hittites, 5
'Holy war', 57, 71
Hosea, 50, 116
Hushai, 92f.
Hyksos, 25

Ishbosheth, 84
Ishmael, Ishmaelites, 11, 29
Israelites, historical origins, 5, 21, 24–6, 58

Jabbok, 22, 93
Jebel Musa, 43
Jehovah 39f.
Jeremiah, 7f.
Jericho, 54–7
Jeroboam, 110
Jerusalem, 84f., 91–3, 97
Jews, physical features, 5
Joab, 93f., 95f., 99
Josephus, 36

Kadesh, 47f.
Koran, 6

INDEX

Kingdom of God, 73
Kiriath-jearim, 85

Levites, 40
LORD, 39f.
Lot, 4, 9f.
Lot, selection by, 69

Mahanaim, 93
Megiddo, 104
Mephibosheth, 86f.
Messianic king, 73, 98
Micah, 13
Midian, Midianites, 29, 37
Moab, Moabites, 11, 103
Moon-worship, 6
Mt Horeb, 37, 41, 43f., 47f.
Mt Sinai, 35, 43f., 47f.

Nathan, 89, 99

Ophir, 107
Old Testament: earliest Hebrew MSS, 76
Greek version, 76
Old Testament narratives and historical fact, 3f., 14, 21, 24–6, 34–6, 44f., 53–8, 64f., 74f., 98, 95, 100, 103f., 106f.

Passover, origins, 41
Philistines, 42, 63, 65, 68–71, 74, 81–3, 85
Prophets, 63f., 73, 111–4
Prophetic ideal of Israelite kingship, 73, 88, 98, 109f.
Proverbs, authorship, 102
Psalms, authorship, 102

Recorder, 97
Red Sea, 35
'Red Sea', 35, 43f.
Rehoboam, 109f.
Religious festivals, Israelite, 41

Sacrifice: first-born animals, 41
first-born son, 13, 41
first-fruits of victory, 57
passover lamb, 42
Christ, 42
Scribe, 97
Semites, 5, 25, 35
Sheba, Queen of, 107
Shechem, 23, 26, 58f.
Sheshonk, 103
Shiloh, 66f.
Shimei, 95f.
Shittim, 52

Tell-el-Damieh, 54
Temple, 85f. 100, 106
Ten Commandments, 49
Terah, 5
Thutmose III, 35
Tribute, 97, 105, 110

Ur of the Chaldees, 5
Uriah, 88f.
Urim and Thummim, 69

Voice of God, 7–9, 67

Wisdom of Amenemope, 103

Yam Sūph, 44

Ziglag, 82

For Product Safety Concerns and Information please contact our EU representative GPSR@taylorandfrancis.com
Taylor & Francis Verlag GmbH, Kaufingerstraße 24, 80331 München, Germany

www.ingramcontent.com/pod-product-compliance
Lightning Source LLC
Chambersburg PA
CBHW061417300426
44114CB00015B/1971